THE
EATER
GUIDE TO
Los Angeles

By the editors of Eater

Illustrations by Clay Hickson

Abrams Image, New York

CONTENTS

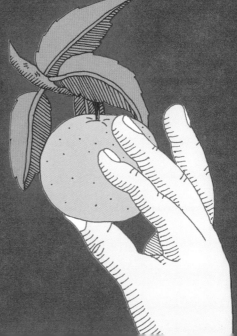

INTRODUCTION

Los Angeles is a city that's symbolic of so many things—of culture, of creativity, of community. It's a global capital that continually redefines itself, which is what makes it so exciting as a food destination. It's a place that, whether purposefully or not, sets dining trends that echo throughout the country and beyond.

Because of this dynamism, Los Angeles was one of the first cities that Eater started covering, way back in 2009. What Eater is today—in-depth restaurant recommendations and news in more than twenty cities, award-winning coverage of national and global dining trends, plus multiple video and TV shows and a line of books—comes from our deep dedication to what we consider the best food cities around the world. LA is vast yet can be understood and contextualized, neighborhood by neighborhood, if you have the right guide. How else can you navigate the red sauce joints of West Hollywood, noodle houses of the San Gabriel Valley, old-school burger spots, K-Town barbecue destinations, mariscos carts and taco stands, and the obscene number of good bakeries this sprawling city has to offer?

Lifelong Angelenos, warm-weather transplants, and countless international and domestic visitors know that it's futile to try to eat your way through the city in one visit. Los Angeles begs for deeper exploration; you could easily spend days tracking down the best Oaxacan food, feasting on Armenian food, or working your way through the endless farmers' markets, street carts, and food trucks. To make the city (somewhat) easier to navigate, we've broken it down into seven major areas, with plenty of context and restaurant and shop recommendations, organized alphabetically. These Eater-approved venues are a mix of enduring icons and newer places that have fundamentally changed the dining scene in some way. So whether you're a first-time visitor who needs a primer for the city, or are looking for a day of eating that starts with a classic diner breakfast and ends with drinking at a Korean restaurant and speakeasy, or want a taste of LA's history through its most iconic Old Hollywood institutions, this guidebook will help you make sense of it all. It was written by our LA-based Eater team, who may just be the world's biggest proponents of the city as the center of the culinary universe.

Let this book inspire your next LA trip, and bring it along so you can take notes as you bop from Santa Monica to Echo Park to downtown LA. The idea of carrying a physical travel guide around might seem a bit antiquated—the phone in your pocket has some version of everything here and more—but information overload and decision fatigue are very real. With this guide, we aimed to distill years of insight and knowledge about Los Angeles to bring you a mix of our always reliable favorites and of-the-moment recommendations, in a travel-friendly format.

If you want even more of our expert-led advice and recommendations, there are QR codes that will take you to maps and guides on the Eater site. This is LA; you already know you'll be spending a decent amount of time traveling from neighborhood to neighborhood—so consider this guidebook your ultimate companion as you figure out where you'll get your next pupusa, boba, or smash burger. It'll make the time stuck in traffic go by that much faster.

— **Amanda Kludt**, publisher, and
Stephanie Wu, editor in chief

Alhambra
Arcadia
City of Industry
Monterey Park
Pasadena
Rosemead
San Gabriel
South El Monte
Temple City

SAN GABR

& PAS

1

HEL VALLEY PASADENA

SAN GABRIEL VALLEY & PASADENA

DINING

1. 101 Noodle Express
2. Agnes Restaurant & Cheesery
3. Bar Chelou
4. Bistro Na's
5. Carnitas El Momo
6. Chef Tony
7. Chengdu Taste
8. Chong Qing Special Noodles
9. Dai Ho Restaurant
10. Delicious Food Corner
11. Din Tai Fung
12. Golden Deli San Gabriel
13. Kogane
14. Lan Noodle
15. Lucky Boy
16. Me + Crêpe
17. Medan Kitchen
18. Newport Seafood Restaurant
19. Old Sasoon Bakery
20. Pie 'n Burger
21. Rodney's Ribs
22. Roma Market
23. Sichuan Impression
24. Su-Beoreg & Monta Factory
25. Tam's Noodle House
26. Union Restaurant
27. Yang's Kitchen

SHOPPING

1. Alhambra Farmers' Market
2. Car Artisan Chocolate
3. Garo's Basturma
4. Gioia Cheese Co.
5. Grist & Toll
6. Jim's Bakery
7. JJ Bakery & Cafe
8. King Kho Bo
9. Little Flower
10. Namaste Spiceland
11. Semolina Artisanal Pasta
12. Vroman's Bookstore

SAN GABRIEL VALLEY & PASADENA
DINING

We start all the way east, in the San Gabriel Valley (aka the SGV) and Pasadena. With the largest concentration of Asian American communities in the country, it's not surprising that the SGV is known for some of the finest Asian restaurants in Southern California, including significant Sichuan, Cantonese, and Vietnamese food scenes. Drive along one of the busy boulevards: Garvey, Valley, Las Tunas, or Baldwin Park, and the eyes will feast on strip mall after strip mall of restaurants wedged in next to one another. But the SGV also offers some surprises, including destination-worthy Mexican, Italian, burgers, and more.

    Meanwhile Pasadena is better known for its idyllic suburban neighborhoods and annual Rose Parade than its culinary offerings. But with a slew of new openings over the past few years and always bustling standbys scattered around town, it has quietly become one of the busiest dining scenes anywhere in Southern California. Both neighborhoods merit the trek east of Downtown.

1. 101 Noodle Express

1408 East Valley Boulevard, Alhambra

Most people come to this Alhambra classic for the beef roll (shown above), a scallion pancake stuffed with thinly sliced beef, cilantro, and sauce, but 101 Noodle Express has a huge menu of other dishes, like dan dan noodles and pan-fried dumplings, that run the gamut of Chinese cuisine. It's a reliable, affordable restaurant good for feeding a crowd.

2. Agnes Restaurant & Cheesery

40 West Green Street, Pasadena

Husband-and-wife team Thomas and Vanessa Tilaka Kalb marry fine cheeses and regional American cooking—taking inspiration from the Midwest, California, and beyond—at this Pasadena restaurant-slash-market that's become a local favorite for brunch, after-work cheese-and-meat boards, and beyond. Grab a seat on the lush twelve-hundred-square-foot patio and have a glass of wine accompanied by handmade pastas and hearth-roasted meats.

3. Bar Chelou

37 South El Molino Avenue, Pasadena

Chef Doug Rankin orchestrates the menu at Bar Chelou, tucked into the scenic courtyard space next to the Pasadena Playhouse. The cooking is ambitious, and not just for Pasadena, with wholly original takes on local produce and the culinary mishmash that is Los Angeles. Think carrots with coconut dressing, lime leaf, and peanuts, but also clam toast with leeks and escabeche, and merguez with green bean tabbouleh. The menu changes constantly, making it a great repeat visit.

4. Bistro Na's

9055 Las Tunas Drive #105, Temple City

Seeing as this opulent destination decked out with gold accents and outfitted with luxe private dining rooms is the only restaurant in the SGV to have been awarded a coveted Michelin star, expect the menu (and prices) to be equally luxurious. The most upscale restaurant in the area is best visited with a group to try large platters of palace-style fare like spicy dry-braised black cod.

5. Carnitas El Momo

1470 Monterey Pass Road, Monterey Park

This former food truck, a citywide favorite for some of the crispiest, juiciest carnitas, now has a stand-alone location in Monterey Park. Their Aporkalypse behemoth is a gluttonous thing of carnal beauty.

6. Chef Tony

1108 South Baldwin Avenue, Arcadia

Taking over the former Din Tai Fung (page 12) space in Arcadia, Chef Tony, conceived by Cantonese chef Tony He, is the smaller-menu cousin of its original Rosemead restaurant Sea Harbour (which is also excellent and appears on page 104). The dim sum offerings, which include He's new-school take on classic bites, are among the best in the SGV. Look for steamed shrimp and scallop dumplings topped with roe.

7. Chengdu Taste

828 West Valley Boulevard, Alhambra

Tony Xu's timeless Sichuan restaurant sometimes packs unrelenting heat into its dishes—but the sensation can be awe-inspiring. The dan dan noodles, mung bean noodles, spicy wontons, toothpick lamb, and eggplant dishes are the highlights at this revered Alhambra spot, which can draw hefty waits during prime mealtimes.

8. Chong Qing Special Noodles

708 East Las Tunas Drive, San Gabriel

The late Jonathan Gold was a tireless supporter of Chong Qing Special Noodles, which is a bit hidden away from San Gabriel's main drag. It's worth finding this spartan noodle shop, which has more types of dishes than three restaurant menus put together, including mapo tofu, fried rice, and twice-cooked pork. As its name would suggest, the noodle soups and flavor-laden dan dan noodles are why you're here.

9. Dai Ho Restaurant

9148 Las Tunas Drive, Temple City

Dai Ho, famous for its delicious Taiwanese beef noodle soup filled with egg noodles, a rich broth, and hunks of stewed meat, is the kind of classic, low-key restaurant that will instantly add street credibility to your LA dining knowledge. Get to the Temple City restaurant early, before anything sells out, and be sure to bring cash.

10. Delicious Food Corner

545 West Las Tunas Drive San Gabriel

This bustling Hong Kong–style café in the predominantly Asian community of Monterey Park on the western edge of the SGV has a huge menu of everyday Cantonese fare, from congee and rice rolls by day to more shareable noodle dishes and stir-fries in the evening. The whole place has the feel of a fast-food diner in Hong Kong, but with immense portions and flavor packed into every grain of fried rice. Bring a crew and order a ton of dishes, like roast duck, honey walnut shrimp, and chow fun.

11. Din Tai Fung

400 South Baldwin Avenue, Arcadia

The SGV was the original landing spot in North America for this Taiwan-based chain, and Din Tai Fung has in recent years expanded and relocated its SGV branch to inside the Shops at Santa Anita. There the iconic restaurant serves Shanghai-influenced xiao long bao (soup dumplings) and stir-fried fare in a high-ceilinged, modern dining room. In addition to dumplings, try the refreshing cold cucumber appetizer, comforting pan-fried rice cakes, and braised beef noodle soup.

12. Golden Deli San Gabriel

815 West Las Tunas Drive San Gabriel

The go-to order at this family-run Vietnamese restaurant (perhaps the best Vietnamese in the SGV) is the crunchy, bubbly cha gio (fried egg rolls) filled with ground pork and served with lettuces and herbs. But the menu is extensive, featuring everything from bun to big bowls of fantastic pho—one of the many reasons one can expect a wait during prime dining hours.

13. Kogane

1129 South Fremont Avenue C, Alhambra

Prepare for a high-end omakase experience at this sleek seven-seat counter in Alhambra, where dinner starts at upwards of $250 and lunch around half that. It's run by two chefs who met by chance in a prep kitchen during the pandemic and are now serving some of the area's most upscale sushi. Dinner might start with appetizers such as gently cooked abalone before moving into sashimi, nigiri, and dishes like seaweed stuffed with San Diego sea urchin.

14. Lan Noodle

411 East Huntington Drive, Arcadia

In the running for the best noodle shop in SGV, Lan Noodle, which also shows up as Lanzhou Beef Noodle in online listings, is a place for incredible spicy hand-made soups and more in a casual strip-mall space. The best ones to order are the wide hand-pulled noodles, dense in the middle but tender on the edges, like

classic dishes such as beef rendang, lemongrass fried chicken, and grilled pork satay in prepackaged take-out dishes.

18. Newport Seafood Restaurant

518 West Las Tunas Drive, San Gabriel

With an expansive Cantonese menu with Cambodian influences, this huge stand-alone building in San Gabriel remains one of the region's top overall restaurants, especially for its oversized platters of fresh lobster stir-fried with green onion and garlic and bo luc lac (shaking beef). The giant portions and above-average prices make this the ideal spot for a big night out with a group.

19. Old Sasoon Bakery

1132 Allen Avenue, Pasadena

Opened by Haroutioun Geragosian in Pasadena in 1986, Old Sasoon Bakery is named after the village in Armenia that his grandparents left after World War II. The beorags (savory hand pies) and the lahmajoun (flatbreads) make for perfect on-the-go eating, but sit down for a well-made khachapuri if time allows. This Georgian breakfast staple comes topped with a blend of cheeses, a single runny egg, and a few pats of melted butter—all in a boat-shaped flatbread.

chewy pasta that just soaks up chile oil and sauce like a sponge. Be sure to ask for things on the spicy side for maximum flavor.

15. Lucky Boy

640 South Arroyo Parkway, Pasadena

No list of places to eat in Pasadena would be complete without the inclusion of Lucky Boy, the city's after-hours greasy spoon take-out joint that makes a killer breakfast burrito. Also on offer are burgers, dogs, tacos, and sandwiches, so really, whatever you're craving after a late evening out. In a city where everything closes early, Lucky Boy is one of the few spots that draws out the night owls.

16. Me + Crêpe

89 East Green Street, Pasadena

Vancouver-based mini chain Me + Crêpe is all about the jianbing, one of China's most popular street foods, consisting of paper-thin pancakes stuffed with things like fried eggs and Beijing duck. The cheery little spot on Pasadena's Green Street also serves tofu soup, pork and shrimp dumplings, and cold and hot soybean milk.

17. Medan Kitchen

8518 Valley Boulevard, Rosemead

Rosemead's hub for Indonesian fare is run by a septuagenarian who became a restaurant owner during the pandemic. Siu Chen, along with two of her daughters, two sons-in-law, and two grandchildren who help run the place, serves

20. Pie 'n Burger

913 East California Boulevard, Pasadena

Pasadena claims to be the birthplace of the cheeseburger, and while the truth of such things is lost to history, there's no denying the enduring prominence of Pie 'n Burger. A legend since 1963, this diner–turned–ode to all things burgers continues to turn out these impeccable California specimens, complete with special sauce and lightly melted American cheese. Don't forget to order a slice of seasonal fruit pie to complete the experience.

21. Rodney's Ribs

902 North Lake Avenue, Pasadena

Catch Rodney Jenkins and his smoker-on-wheels Tuesdays through Saturdays at the CVS parking lot on North Lake in Pasadena. This pop-up is open for lunch and dinner and serves outstanding pork ribs and beef brisket sandwiches that are smoked on-site. The portions are big, the sandwiches are saucy, and the sides, like mac and cheese and baked beans, are plentiful.

22. Roma Market

918 North Lake Avenue, Pasadena

The reason to come to this Pasadena deli is to try "The Sandwich," which consists of a sturdy Italian roll drizzled with olive oil, sprinkled with salt, and layered with provolone, mortadella, spiced coppa, and salami. It's renowned for its simple and satisfying prowess—and is the only sandwich the market serves. If you're lucky, octogenarian owner Rosario Mazzeo might be hanging out on a chair barking orders or greeting customers.

23. Sichuan Impression

235 West Main Street, Alhambra

One of the two main Sichuan restaurant powerhouses in the SGV, Alhambra's Sichuan Impression serves polished regional dishes with enough spice to draw a decent amount of sweat on the brow. Start with the cold house special noodles, dressed in chili oil and vinegar. End with a plate of fried intestines or a fiery bowl of mapo tofu laced with Sichuan chiles. Check out the West LA location, too.

24. Su-Beoreg & Monta Factory

1531 East Washington Boulevard, Pasadena

Come to this homey family-owned shop in Pasadena for two Armenian specialties: su beoreg and sini-monta. Think of su beoreg like a lasagna—layers of thin, house-made dough complemented with feta, mozzarella, and chopped parsley. Buy a whole pan or snag a slice. The sini-monta (shown above) are open-faced beef dumplings seasoned with sumac and red pepper and slathered with spicy pepper paste and a tangy yogurt-based garlic cream sauce.

25. Tam's Noodle House

120 North San Gabriel Boulevard, San Gabriel

Tam's Noodle House in San Gabriel serves Hong Kong– and Cantonese-style café foods like curry with fish balls, barbecue pork, beef stew lo mein, steamed rice roll, and Hong Kong–style milk tea. All the noodles and dumplings are made in-house. Tam's offers three varieties of noodles, including wonton-style egg

QR CODES
for our online guides to these neighborhoods:

PASADENA

SAN GABRIEL VALLEY

noodles, rice noodles, and flat egg noodles. It's one of the places in SGV that feels plucked right out of a busy Hong Kong street.

26. Union Restaurant
37 Union Street,
Pasadena

Chef Christopher Keyser prepares some of the best plates of pasta in town at Pasadena's tiny-but-mighty Union Restaurant, located in Old Pasadena. Twisty torchetti come topped with a spicy Calabrese pork ragu, while the squid ink lumache plays well with Maine lobster and truffle butter, and the tonnarelli cacio e pepe is topped with a soft egg (shown above). It's the kind of dream Italian American restaurant everyone wants to have in their neighborhood.

27. Yang's Kitchen
112 West Main Street,
Alhambra

A modern Asian American restaurant with seasonal ingredients and chef-driven, California-inspired fare, Yang's Kitchen is committed to impeccable ingredient sourcing and providing living wages for its workers. For those dining at the Alhambra destination for brunch or lunch, the plate-sized pancake made with blue cornmeal and mochiko flour makes for an awesomely chewy short stack. The dish to get on the dinner menu is the chile butter–glazed Hainanese fish rice, made with dry-aged barramundi and served with chicken-fat rice, ginger-scallion sauce, and pickled cucumbers.

SAN GABRIEL VALLEY & PASADENA
SHOPPING

The forty-seven neighborhoods within this sprawling suburban community each have their own unique history and vibe, from San Gabriel's Spanish architecture to San Marino's well-manicured parks and Pasadena's idyllic Craftsman homes. Sweeping views of the San Gabriel mountains north of the region give way to wide boulevards, plentiful strip malls, and bustling commerce. The diverse shopping options reflect the richness of residents' cultures and traditions, offering Armenian-style cured meat, world-class bean-to-bar chocolates, fresh Italian cheese, and more.

1. Alhambra Farmers' Market

100 South 2nd Street, Alhambra

Find the season's best locally grown fruits and vegetables, along with herbs, honeys, and bread, at the Alhambra farmers' market, held every Sunday from eight thirty A.M. to one P.M. Given the community's large Asian population, the selection of produce includes local favorites like winter melon, loofah, bitter melon, leafy greens like morning glory and bok choy, and tropical fruits like dragon fruit and mangosteens.

2. Car Artisan Chocolate

1009 East Colorado Boulevard, Pasadena

Haris Car is dedicated to producing chocolate from bean to bar using sustainably sourced cacao at this Pasadena-based manufactory and café. Car's line of chocolate bars begins with cacao beans grown on farms in South America and Africa that pay their farmers high premiums. The chocolates are minimally processed on-site to highlight each origin's unique flavor profile. The café serves drinking chocolates, as well as coffee-cocoa mash-ups that provide a substantial caffeine buzz.

3. Garo's Basturma

1082 Allen Avenue, Pasadena

While Pasadena's Armenian population isn't as robust as neighboring Glendale's, the contingent is large enough to support many excellent Armenian businesses, including Garo's Basturma. The deli/grocer has been making its namesake cured meat and selling it by the pound for nearly forty years. While lesser-quality basturma can be a bit chewy and dry, the expertly cured wares at Garo's are meltingly tender with a delicate crust of fenugreek, cumin, black pepper, and paprika.

4. Gioia Cheese Co.

1605 Potrero Avenue, South El Monte

Burrata cheese is a mainstay on many menus across the city thanks to Gioia Cheese, a San Gabriel Valley–based factory dedicated to making the best fresh mozzarella in town. This small operation in South El Monte produces two thousand pounds daily using old-world Italian techniques passed on through generations of the Girardi family. The factory's products are available for sale to the public Monday, Tuesday, Thursday, and Friday on a walk-in basis.

5. Grist & Toll

990 South Arroyo Parkway, Pasadena

As the first urban flour mill in Los Angeles in almost a century, Pasadena's Grist & Toll is dedicated to local, small-batch, and wholegrain milled flours. Grist & Toll's line of flours include whole rye, spelt, and hard and soft white, as well as polenta and cornmeal. In addition to providing many of the city's bakeries and restaurants with its top-of-the-line products, the Pasadena mill is open to the public Wednesday through Saturday from eleven A.M. to five P.M. to satisfy all home baking needs.

6. Jim's Bakery

400 South Atlantic Boulevard, Monterey Park

San Gabriel Valley denizens have been coming into Jim's Bakery for Hong Kong–style pastries for the past three decades. Opened in 1991 by Oscar Jim, the sweets shop is a neighborhood staple for its matchless Hong Kong and Portuguese egg tarts (shown on page 18). While the former includes a sweet egg custard filling and shortbread crust, the latter brings together caramelized custard cradled in puff pastry. Both are baked throughout the day, are served comfortingly warm, and travel exceedingly well.

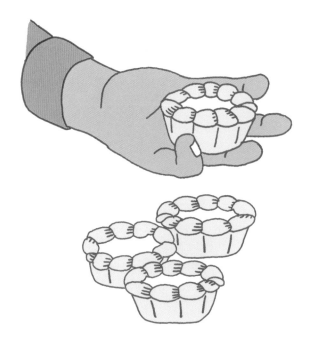

9. Little Flower
1424 West Colorado Boulevard, Pasadena

Former restaurant pastry chef Christine Moore's scratch-made caramels and marshmallows are the stuff of legend. Here in her cozy café on the edge of town, Moore makes pillowy marshmallows coated in sheaths of granulated sugar in flavors like vanilla, cinnamon-sugar, coffee, and chocolate. The lemon, vanilla, and sea salt caramels are equally dazzling and packaged in bundles to go or sold one by one from a jar near the cash register.

10. Namaste Spiceland
270 North Hill Avenue, Pasadena

Part grocery store and part fast-casual eatery, Namaste Spiceland is an excellent resource for South Asian food. Groceries range from bulk bags of basmati rice to jarred spices and chutneys intended for home cooks. The smell of prepared Indian food wafts through the narrow aisles, beckoning shoppers to sit down for a bite of southern and northern specialties like pav bhaji (vegetable curry served with a roll) and gulab jamun (fried dough balls soaked in syrup).

7. JJ Bakery & Cafe
18558 Gale Avenue, City of Industry

Founded in 1996, this Taiwanese shop bakes a tremendous line of sweet and savory pastries, including cakes of all stripes and plush buns filled with things like cheese, corn, pork floss, and even hot dogs—most of which come individually wrapped. Visit the flagship location in City of Industry or the one in Arcadia for Taiwanese breakfast items like soy milk and scallion pancakes, in addition to the usual selection of baked goods. Find additional locations in Hacienda Heights, Rowland Heights, Torrance, and Temple City.

8. King Kho Bo
1621 South San Gabriel Boulevard, San Gabriel

Stock up on Vietnamese-style beef jerky (kho bo), dried fruit, and candies at this independently owned store a stone's throw from the San Gabriel Superstore, a massive, can't-miss-it Asian supermarket. The shop's affable owner puts newcomers at ease while they navigate the plethora of jerky options on hand. Wares are priced and sold by weight.

11. Semolina Artisanal Pasta

1976-1978 Lincoln Avenue, Pasadena

Leah Ferrazzani began making fresh and dried pastas from her home in 2014 and has since expanded her operation into a brick-and-mortar in Pasadena. The pastas made on-site are delivered to local restaurants like Yang's Kitchen in Alhambra (page 15) and Hippo in Highland Park (page 36), as well as retailers big and small. The shop on Lincoln Avenue carries Semolina's entire line of pastas, along with fresh and jarred sauces, cheeses, and olive oils.

12. Vroman's Bookstore

695 East Colorado Boulevard, Pasadena

It's unsurprising to think that Southern California's oldest bookstore is the place to come for cookbooks, food lit, and more, especially works by local authors. But it also stocks a huge array of gifty items, including those for your kitchen and table (coasters, tea strainers, linens, and the like). The massive building also boasts 1883, a craft beer, wine, and "literary themed cocktail bar" tucked inside the entrance, the ideal pairing for some relaxed page-turning.

BEYOND RESTAURANTS

Coffee Shops:
AK Fresh Roast
Café Santo
Copa Vida
Mandarin Coffee
    Stand

Bars:
Angel and Mason
The Blind Donkey
Progress on Main
The Speakeasy

Bakeries:
Kee Wah Bakery
Oh My Pan
Olympic Bakery
Seed Bakery

Ice Cream:
Afters Ice Cream
Fair Oaks Pharmacy
Fosselman's Ice Cream
    Co.

A BRIEF HISTORY OF DINING IN LA

By Farley Elliott

The story of food in Los Angeles is akin to the city itself: endlessly sprawling and meaning many different things to different people. What makes LA so special is that it is truly a choose-your-own-adventure place to live and eat. Glance at a map, and what first appears to be a giant mass of land becomes illuminated and vibrant when you look closer and find the pockets that speak to you. Los Angeles is everything at once, a region north of eighteen million people that offers the old and the new, fine dining and fast food, at every turn.

The region's rich tradition of agriculture and fishing and trade extends back hundreds of years and continues on today, at lively city street food stands, deep in the area's complex suburbs, and along the sandy shores of the Pacific Ocean. The first peoples of greater Los Angeles were the Gabrielino/Tongva and Chumash, among many others, and they spent their years moving toward and away from the ocean depending on the season. Far from the desert it is sometimes derisively described to be, Los Angeles was (and in many ways still is) a temperate coastal Mediterranean-like valley rich with trees and grass, perfect for foraging and hunting in addition to all that fishing. In time, the population began to grow inland along the rivers, a protective decision made to keep Spanish, Portuguese, and other European explorers at least somewhat at bay (consider that Downtown Los Angeles is miles from the ocean's shore), while also expanding the grape-growing and cattle-grazing opportunities that began to flood in with Spanish and Mexican settlers.

The earliest rancheros and vaqueros, beginning in earnest in the 1700s, readily embraced inland life, laying claim to huge

land grants across the Los Angeles basin. From Orange County through Santa Barbara, cattlemen would move their herds with the seasons, relying on pit-smoked sides of beef, cured linguica sausages (thank you, Portuguese settlers), and pinquito beans to feed them. Lesser-used scrap cuts of beef—the preferred animal protein, owing to the abundance of grazing land that allowed for such a robust cattle industry—could also be salted, seasoned, grilled, and lightly smoked to a rosy interior, marking the beginnings of the Santa Maria–style tri-tip barbecue (a style known for cooking the triangular cut of beef from the cow's hindquarter over coastal red oak) that has become so well-known along the Central Coast.

The Ortega family would found its now-ubiquitous salsa and pepper company in the young town of Ventura in the 1890s (two decades before California's statehood), relying on a strain of New Mexico chiles to make its famed sauces. A steep increase in agricultural production coincided with the region's population boom and the growth of the Ortega Chili Company overall, and by the early 1900s other big names like El Pato—today a staple on store shelves across the country, known for its bright colors and vintage duck logo—had further entered the salsa, pickled pepper, and sauce market.

In the Los Angeles basin, wine was fast becoming a boomtown commodity, with more than one hundred vineyards dotting the hillsides and valleys by 1850. Grapevines were first brought by Spanish settlers and, famously, Franciscan missionaries at sites like the San Gabriel Mission, where vines were planted in the 1700s and can still be found today. The center of town was bustling, too. Formally founded as "El Pueblo de Nuestra Señora la Reina de Los Ángeles del Rio de la Porciúncula" by Sonorans and Native Americans in 1781, Los Angeles had by the late 1800s become a traveler's destination, spurred on by not one but two rail lines connecting LA with points farther east. The city's population would double twice over between 1890 and 1905, jumping from fifty thousand to two hundred thousand strong. In the center of town, ad hoc markets sprung up selling every-thing from land deeds to building supplies to tamales, leaving early travelers to wonder in diaries and dispatches home whether or not LA even offered indoor dining.

A Chinatown stood not far from the central plaza (near LA's current Chinatown), with the dense neigh-borhood acting as a haven for newly arrived immigrants, many of whom faced outsized discrimination and poor working conditions in mines and on railroad construction crews. Despite the often-brutal living con-ditions—in 1871 a racially motivated massacre in the community spurred on by mostly white landowners led to the shooting or hanging of 10 percent of Chinatown's population—small Chinese-owned medicine shops, groceries, and takeaway food options proliferated, with vendors often selling their wares alongside tamaleros (makers of tamales, the iconic steamed corn husks stuffed with masa and other fillings) on the city's main avenues. As white settlers continued to pour into Los Angeles on the brand-new trains, some in search of gold, others in search of clean air and cheap land, govern-ment officials began to ostracize and criminalize street vendors. Though as anyone who has spent any time in Los Angeles knows, the century-plus campaign has yielded few

results except for occasional bouts of intimidation and harassment. Street vendors are a historic and important part of the dining landscape here. Always have been, always will be.

The real restaurant explosion for Los Angeles began around the turn of the twentieth century, coinciding with the region's massive popula-tion growth. New business centers began, in turn, to draw in street vendors, restaurateurs, and market owners eager to capitalize on the area's growing density. Philippe The Original (just Philippe's, locally; page 69) opened downtown in 1908, serving a variety of breakfast and casual deli items to workers and locals before eventually launching the French dip sandwich. In 1917, Grand Central Market opened at the base of Bunker Hill, then considered an upscale community for home-owners with business interests nearby. The market, open on two sides, was meant to be a one-stop shop for the workers and homemak-ers who lived up the hill, offering butcher services, produce vendors, and more, all in a single easy-to-access location—and, of course, city officials hoped that the whites-only market would help to further drive out pushcart vendors selling goods and foods on those very same streets. While not initially a hub for cooked meals served at small vendor stalls like it is today (more on that later—see page 46), the market nevertheless anchored downtown as a place where quality food could be had. The same is true today.

In 1929, Olvera Street (page 74) opened as a kind of living homage to the city's past. Laid atop what was previously known as historic Vine Street (because of the old vineyards nearby), the walkable stretch had indeed been one of the city's earliest thoroughfares, but without the sellers, splashy colors, and food vendors that have come to populate it today. Tourists were attracted even then to images of the old LA, complete with sagging adobe structures and rutty laneways. A small, orange-toned stand at one end, Cielito Lindo, began selling rolled and fried tacos with a thin guacamole sauce just five years later, which have been touted by many as the original taquitos; today the restaurant is a must-visit for a new generation of tourists still drawn to a forgotten LA time.

The Second Great Migration doubled California's Black population in a decade as families relocated from the South in search of social justice and equitable work opportunities—often struggling to find both in the still-segregated state. That led to a humongous influx of Southern, soul food, and other regional cooking styles. Black families brought familiar foods, from Southern and Texas-style barbecue to Louisiana Cajun and Creole dishes to West African soups and spices, often jumping from home-cooking enterprises to full-fledged restaurants to serve a growling clientele. As the historic and enduring center of Black life, many of these businesses collected in what is today called South Los Angeles—a term that roughly covers a swath of the county between the 10 freeway and Long Beach, east of the coastline, an area larger than the island of Manhattan. Today its neighborhoods and standalone cities make up the epicenter for many of these foods, including shrimp and grits, Southern-style fried chicken, collard greens, and grilled chicken sausage links.

LA's rapid growth during this time literally paved the way for highways, new towns, and an often racially motivated de-urbanization movement (combined with redlining and other discriminatory covenants that defined where many nonwhites could live) that pushed people out into the suburbs. Perhaps more so than any other major metropolitan area in America, Los Angeles is both a city, densely populated and welcoming, and a collection of communities, neighborhoods, and distinctly suburban areas linked together by freeways and rail lines. There is no Los Angeles without its suburbs, and there are no suburbs without fast-food stands, restaurant chains, and strip malls—all immensely important to the way that Angelenos eat.

The decades after World War II led to uncompromising growth in Southern California, an ever-widening effect that touched on nearly every aspect of life, from agriculture and water to shipping and streetlights. The original 1940s-era McDonald's, located in San Bernardino years before Ray Kroc came along, helped to popularize the idea of fast food and pushed people to rethink both the cost and convenience of their meals. The Snyder family behind the California-famous In-N-Out Burger chain, meanwhile, introduced the first two-way speaker box in 1948, further moving the crowds from carhop setups and small outdoor tables to true drive-thru decadence. Within a decade, diners could find themselves motoring on newly finished streets from their downtown offices to a pickup window selling hamburgers

and shakes, minutes before pulling up to a brand-new subdivision home shaded by palm trees.

The story of modern American food, then, is really a story of Los Angeles. Carl's Jr. was founded here (1941), Winchell's Donut House was founded here (1948), and Hot Dog on a Stick was founded here (1946), alongside Wienerschnitzel (1961). The rise of interstate highways meant more commerce, more commodity beef, and more access for the average American to a diet and a lifestyle that had previously been impossible to imagine, let alone afford. Midwestern cows could be slaughtered by midday and shipped to Los Angeles in time to make the opening shift the following morning. Pastrami—thinly shaved and served in heaps over fries, on top of burgers, or even inside wrapped tortillas, a unique Los Angeles convention— and ground beef became staples on LA's fast-food menus, inviting newcomers like Fatburger (1952) to try their hand at mass meat marketing.

Among the most formidable names to come out of this era of Angeleno food dominance is Taco Bell, founded by Glen Bell in 1962 in the city's suburbs. Bell had previously tried his hand at hot dogs, so the legend goes, before noticing that a restaurant across the street from his stand was doing brisk business selling hard-shelled tacos with shredded cheese and a spiced ground beef mixture. Having befriended the owners, Bell took the dish and simplified it for an on-the-go audience, moving the tacos from diner plates to paper bags. The originator, Mitla Cafe, is still open in San Bernardino, while Glen Bell made countless millions from the taco that he is said to have taken. The massive Taco Bell Corporation is now located not far away in Irvine, California.

In forthcoming years, Los Angeles's unique brand of dining would come to dominate American culture. Television shows and movies and songs glorified the so-called Old Hollywood, with Rat Pack types hanging out at Italian American dinner spots, lounge clubs, or sit-down Mexican restaurants, sipping drinks and smoking. At Lawry's The Prime Rib, servers in suits spun salads tableside, while at Dal Rae it was possible to sit at an eating rail bolted directly to the baby grand piano, all the better for catching the action up close.

Los Angeles even helped to perfect and grow the American diner (often called "coffee shops" locally), leaning into novelty architecture styles, such as the funky, space-age-inspired Googie, as part of the kitsch. Opened in 1949 and now boasting more than twenty locations across Southern California, the twenty-four-hour diner Norms is the classic LA breakfast chain, but Denny's, IHOP, and even Sizzler were all founded here—and so, too, was Cheesecake Factory, back in 1972. Together all of these chains, from Taco Bell to McDonald's to Orange Julius to Denny's, came to create a corporate pastiche that became the default view of suburban American living for so many. Even today, these multinational brands represent a version of the United States that, while not altogether favorable, is also not entirely inaccurate.

To really understand LA's suburbs today, one must touch on the Immigration and Naturalization Act of 1965, which removed the federal suppression of large numbers of immigrant groups primarily from Asia. The rescission of the Hart-Celler Act remade large swaths of Southern California in a matter of years, growing sections of East Hollywood into enclaves for first-generation Thai families or allowing resettled Cambodians to create impactful communities in Long Beach.

Los Angeles is home to some of the globe's largest expat populations of Vietnamese, Thai, Korean, Filipino, and Armenian people, spread across the city and its surrounding counties, but also compacted into dense immigrant communities that serve as welcoming hubs for new arrivals. The sauce most of us know as Sriracha was born here, created by a Vietnamese immigrant riffing on a Thai chili sauce; the Huy Fong Foods corporation that makes the sought-after stuff is named for the boat that first brought founder David Tran to California's shores. All-hours food and party district Koreatown, in the heart of the city, is today the densest dining neighborhood in all of Los Angeles, with restaurants stacked atop one another in business parks, strip malls, and on street corners. Immigrant food is everywhere, an indelible part of dining out here.

Farther east, nearly two million residents now call the greater San Gabriel Valley home, with more than a quarter of them hailing from Asia. Despite facing untold discrimination and harassment since starting to arrive more than a century ago, Chinese and Taiwanese immigrants have come to dominate the landscape in what's become known simply as the SGV, offering dozens of regional cuisine styles spread across thousands of restaurants. For boba, dumplings, Beijing duck, dim sum, noodle soups, Sichuan peppercorns, beef rolls, and walnut shrimp (among endless other things to eat), the San Gabriel Valley is the place to be, and is arguably the heart of Chinese food in America. And for those craving a little orange chicken, don't forget: Panda Express was founded in Glendale by a San Gabriel family, too, back in 1983.

The 1980s were in some sense a time of rapid change for Los Angeles. The region had gone from being a city full of unrealized potential to becoming a major player on the American restaurant scene in just a matter of decades, seeking to reassert itself beyond fast food and national chains. A small number of dedicated chefs, mostly collected west of downtown, began to formalize a new style of California cuisine, marrying the freshest possible ingredients from local ocean waters and nearby growers in the San Joaquin Valley.

Michael's (page 102), a still-gorgeous indoor-outdoor, ingredient-driven restaurant located just blocks away from the ocean in Santa Monica, was first on the scene in 1979 (though a full eight years after Chez Panisse opened in the Bay Area) and quickly became a hub for young, hungry culinary talents like Jonathan Waxman, Nancy Silverton,

Grill on the Alley (a hub for Hollywood power players to poke at arugula salads) opened alongside Border Grill (where Mary Sue Milliken and Susan Feniger sought to reshape California-Mexican cuisine) and California Pizza Kitchen launched as well. It was Ed LaDou, the pizza chef at Spago known for putting unique ingredients on his pies, who crafted CPK's first menu, and with it the restaurant's true masterpiece—the barbecue chicken pizza.

and the late Mark Peel. The latter two chefs would go on to open Campanile together a decade later—and with it, Silverton's La Brea Bakery, now available nationwide. In 1982, Austrian-born chef Wolfgang Puck opened the first Spago (page 115) as a freewheeling place for celebrities to party over plates of asparagus and smoked salmon pizza. The restaurant was a bit of both worlds: decadent in its clientele and sordid stories, but simplistic in its approach to fine-dining food. Puck's own charisma helped to expand California cuisine nationally, and his face now appears on everything from soup cans to kitchen equipment from coast to coast. In South LA, Simply Wholesome opened in 1984 with much the same goal in mind, providing quality California food for a health-conscious Black audience, albeit in a much more laid-back setting. And in 1985 alone,

Angelenos embraced it all, eager to jump into California cuisine's few-rules approach to dining. As has always been the case, LA diners prefer to keep things casual, opting for sunlit patios and sandals over (for the most part) white tablecloths and broiled steak and potatoes. Still, a few notable true fine-dining restaurants have emerged over the past several decades, including Santa Monica's Mélisse, a Michelin-rated tasting menu spot founded in 1999 by spiky-haired surfer chef Josiah Citrin (page 146). Six years later, Michael Cimarusti would open Providence (page 92) as a temple to sustainable seafood, wrapped in decadent service and elegant pours of wine. Both restaurants have become fine-dining hallmarks for the city, and show just how versatile LA really is.

California cuisine's biggest step forward, though, would come in the early 2000s thanks (in part) to a familiar name: Nancy Silverton. Her Mozza group (page 104), now an empire with outposts all over the globe, was founded on Melrose Avenue, right where Hollywood meets tony Hancock Park, in 2007 as an ode to both California and Italy. The restaurant would go on to help redefine pizza, pasta, regional Italian cooking, and Cal-Ital (for California-Italian, naturally). Over on hip Fairfax, a street known as much for cult streetwear shops as classic Jewish restaurants like Canter's Deli (page 89), Jon Shook and Vinny Dotolo opened their meaty restaurant Animal in 2008 (which closed in 2023), becoming among the first restaurants to institute "no substitutions" policies on its menus while blasting punk and hip-hop at elevated levels in the dining room. The pair—for better and worse—helped to usher in an age of the chef as all-knowing auteur, a culinary mastermind who can rise through the ranks of *Top Chef* to take on the world. Their restaurant group now operates more than half a dozen restaurants and markets around Los Angeles, while also acting as culinary ambassadors to SoFi Stadium (home to the Los Angeles Rams and Chargers) and pulling in millions in annual catering gigs.

The year 2008 was also the year of Roy Choi, who emerged from a career in hotels and other more upscale establishments to create Kogi, a Korean-Mexican fusion food truck that first delivered the Korean taco to America. Choi's hometown pride and bold flavor-on-flavor menu pushed California cuisine to its natural limits, marrying his classic French techniques with Asian and Mexican influences, all served from the same kind of roving street-food setup that has been looked down upon or outright banned in greater Los Angeles since the city's very founding.

We should also note here the importance of Jonathan Gold to the Los Angeles dining scene. Gold was a music journalist–turned–foremost chronicler of all the city's most delicious foods. His stories, reviews, and radio appearances spoke to the dining habits of real Angelenos, in strip malls and outer suburbs and on menus that bore no English writing at all. Gold's "Counter Intelligence" column for *LA Weekly* (which later moved to the *Los Angeles Times*) began in 1986, and his book of the same name was published in 2000. Along the way, Gold ate at every restaurant along Pico Boulevard from Downtown to the ocean, and spoke of chefs, cooks, workers, and hungry late-night crowds with the kind of written reverence usually reserved for celebrities and nobles. In 2007 Gold became the first person to ever win a Pulitzer Prize for food writing, and he remains the city's patron saint of good eats and thoughtful conversations around the way that Angelenos enjoy their food. He died in 2018 at the age of fifty-seven from pancreatic cancer, and in many ways the city still mourns.

Given the rich history of eating in Los Angeles, it follows that there is much to look forward to. A whole new crop of tech-minded companies are rethinking plant-based meat here, or reconceptualizing chain restaurant kitchens with burger-flipping robots or brand deals with YouTube celebrities. It's not always pretty, but it does represent at least a version of where American commodity food is headed.

Meanwhile, Downtown's Grand Central Market (page 67) has not only survived but thrived, acting today as a culinary incubator for celebrated young restaurants. Chefs from lauded food cities (think Enrique Olvera from Mexico City's Pujol, or Stephanie Izard of Chicago's Girl & the Goat) have planted flags here, and collectively they're helping to turn more heads toward Los Angeles than ever before.

Nearby Riverside County has even become a legal safe haven for fully licensed at-home restaurants, ensuring that this newest generation of up-and-coming cooks can continue to thrive and innovate without needing millions of dollars just to get started. There are still legal hurdles for vendors to clear, but civic leaders and supporters alike agree that the food they serve is not only important, but necessary.

It all comes back to street food, of course, the heart and soul of this city's dining culture since its very first days. For hundreds of years, passionate workers and owners have made LA the most diverse, flavorful, and exciting restaurant city in America. And thanks to their ongoing ingenuity and belief in LA's endlessly hungry diners, the city's food future is as bright as ever.

Atwater Village
Boyle Heights
Eagle Rock
East Hollywood
East LA
Echo Park
Highland Park
Los Feliz
Silver Lake
Thai Town

EAST

2

SIDE

EASTSIDE

DINING

1. Al & Bea's Mexican Food
2. All Day Baby
3. Bar Moruno
4. Birrieria Nochistlán
5. Botanica Restaurant & Market
6. Burritos La Palma
7. Cafe Tropical
8. Cosa Buona
9. El Huarache Azteca
10. Goldburger
11. Hippo
12. Jeff's Table
13. Joy
14. Kismet
15. Los Cinco Puntos
16. Lupe's #2
17. Mariscos Jalisco
18. Otomisan
19. Otoño
20. Ototo
21. Pijja Palace
22. Pine & Crane
23. Quarter Sheets Pizza
24. Rosty
25. Spoon & Pork
26. Thunderbolt
27. Tsubaki
28. Valerie Echo Park
29. Villa's Tacos

SHOPPING

1. Bar Keeper
2. Besties Vegan Paradise
3. Bhan Kanom Thai
4. Cookbook
5. El Mercadito
6. Friends & Family
7. La Azteca Tortilleria
8. Le Bon Garçon
9. Maciel's Plant-Based Butcher Shop
10. Milkfarm
11. Sara's Market
12. Silverlake Wine
13. Wine + Eggs
14. Yolk

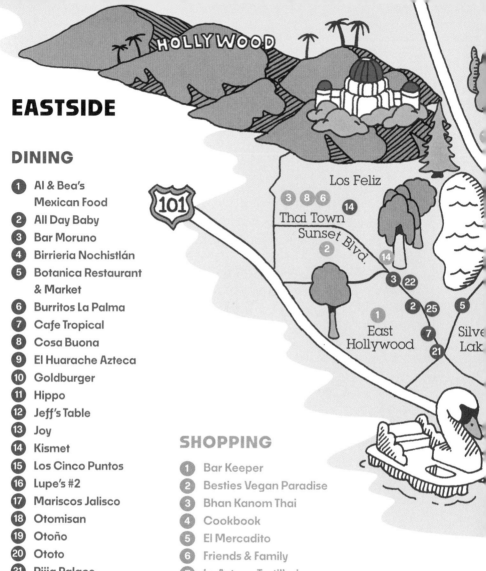

EASTSIDE
DINING

While the term "Eastside" in Los Angeles is used to refer to basically any neighborhood that doesn't touch the ocean, historically speaking it is reserved for the communities directly east of the Los Angeles River, which runs alongside Downtown. Lincoln Heights, for example, is the oldest neighborhood in the city and was once called "East Los Angeles." Other vibrant and historic areas include the predominantly Mexican American communities of El Sereno, Boyle Heights, City Terrace, and what is now broadly referred to as East Los Angeles.

For the purposes of this guidebook, we're also pulling in the neighborhoods just west of Dodger Stadium, Echo Park and Silver Lake—two ever-evolving areas that for years have been churning out some of the most exciting new dining destinations in all of LA. In these trendy enclaves, you'll find third-wave coffee shops and clusters of independent boutiques like those found in Silver Lake's Sunset Junction. Even farther northeast is the rapidly changing Highland Park, a historically Mexican neighborhood where there's still excellent homestyle Mexican food, as well as vintage furniture shops, stylish boutiques, and cavernous modern eateries along its main thoroughfares of York Boulevard and Figueroa Street.

Across the Eastside, you'll find tacos of all kinds and old-school Japanese fare, iconic breakfast spots and Spanish newcomers, veteran burger joints and lively mariscos trucks.

1. Al & Bea's Mexican Food

2025 1st Street,
Boyle Heights

Opened in 1966, this legendary family-owned Boyle Heights restaurant, an order-at-the-counter joint with a few outside tables, serves tremendous bean-and-cheese burritos that were immortalized by the late food writer Jonathan Gold. However, the Mexican American community has revered this roadside stand and neighborhood fixture since the beginning.

2. All Day Baby

3200 Sunset Boulevard,
Silver Lake

A casual corner restaurant outfitted with giant windows, red awnings, and a welcoming bakery case up front, Lien Ta and Jonathan Whitener's second restaurant together (their first being Koreatown's popular Here's Looking at You) screams comfort. A biscuit breakfast sandwich and French toast with crispy ham share daytime menu space with a stellar fried chicken sandwich (shown opposite), a barbacoa burrito, and a hot catfish sandwich with bread-and-butter pickles. The bar next door serves fun cocktails like boozy slushies and updated takes on classic drinks.

3. Bar Moruno

3705 Sunset Boulevard,
Silver Lake

Chef Chris Feldmeier's restaurant done up in hues of mustard and olive green has been drawing raves for its refreshing gin and tonics and flawlessly executed Spanish fare since it reopened in a corner brick building on Sunset Boulevard in early 2022. Sidle up to the long, mirrored bar for little bites like a chorizo-stuffed Scotch egg or white anchovy with guindilla pepper, olives, and shaved cured egg yolk, or settle in at a yellow banquette under vintage Spanish posters for bigger dishes like a whole roasted fish with fried bread and greens.

4. Birrieria Nochistlán

3200 East 4th Street,
Boyle Heights

This simple Boyle Heights spot with bright orange walls and tables outfitted with metal folding chairs serves a homey rendition of braised goat birria in stock made from the drippings with substantial corn tortillas and only a hot chile de árbol salsa, chopped onions, and cilantro as condiments.

5. Botanica Restaurant & Market

1620 Silver Lake Boulevard,
Silver Lake

Opened by two former food journalists in 2017, Botanica has become an essential addition to Silver Lake. The restaurant and marketplace's pale pink walls, healthy-living ethos, excellent baked goods, Mediterranean-inflected dishes like lamb ribs with house-made yogurt, and sunny back patio vibes resonate at brunch and beyond.

6. Burritos La Palma

2811 East Olympic Boulevard,
Boyle Heights

Known for having some of the finest flour tortillas in Los Angeles (which really means in the entire country), Burritos La Palma's entire menu shines, especially the birria, which is juicy and particularly satisfying stuffed inside a quesadilla. All of the must-order burritos at this counter-service destination, with multiple locations across the Eastside and SGV, are filled with succulent stewed meat or beans and cheese.

7. Cafe Tropical

2900 Sunset Boulevard,
Silver Lake

Cafe Tropical, Silver Lake's indomitable Cuban corner restaurant, set up shop next to an iconic bar, the

Silverlake Lounge, back in 1975. Even after four decades, the beloved bakery and restaurant decked out with colorful lights continues to crank out dependably good guava pasteles, Cubanos, media-noche sandwiches, and cafés con leche for the local community.

8. Cosa Buona
2100 Sunset Boulevard, Silver Lake

What's not to love about puffy-crusted pizza, chicken parm, and mozza-rella sticks? It's all possible at chef Zach Pollack's busy pizzeria, Cosa Buona, right on the corner of Sunset and Alvarado in Silver Lake. The tight spot stays bustling most days, with groups sipping natural wine and sharing chopped salads in modern leather booths enveloped in light wood. Check out Pollack's date-night favorite, Alimento, also in Silver Lake.

9. El Huarache Azteca
5225 York Boulevard, Highland Park

The Mexico City–style anto-jitos or "little whims" served at this neighborhood gem in Highland Park are perfect at any time of day. The name-sake huaraches, deep-fried rafts made of masa dough and topped with things like huitlacoche (corn smut), head cheese, and chorizo, never fail to satisfy.

10. Goldburger
5623 York Boulevard, Highland Park

Consistently rated one of the best burgers in a city that truly loves its burgers, Goldburger is known for grass-fed, smashed-style patties done with precision, thoughtful topping combinations, and a punchy house-made garlic aioli. Oh, the beloved Highland Park burger window serves pie and curly fries, too. Ditto the Los Feliz branch on Vermont Avenue.

11. Hippo
5916½ North Figueroa Street, Highland Park

The plates at lively, Italian-leaning Hippo (located in the former Highland Park post office building along with other neighbor-hood favorites like Triple Beam Pizza) are smartly composed with seasonal influences and well-sourced ingredients. The handmade pastas at this cavernous restaurant with an open kitchen and exposed wood-beam ceiling are particu-larly excellent, especially the parcels filled with corn during summer months.

12. Jeff's Table
5900 North Figueroa Street, Highland Park

Jewish deli sandwich lovers will get a kick out of Jeff's Table, a semi-hidden counter at the back of a Highland Park market and liquor store. There, a former Hollywood producer serves new-school takes on roast beef, hot pastrami, and more. The Jeff's Special is a showstopper with hand-sliced pastrami, sauerkraut, Russian dressing, and melted Comté cheese on seeded rye.

13. Joy
5100 York Boulevard, Highland Park

Taiwanese specialist Joy delivers on all fronts, from food to service and ambience (think: exposed brick walls, hanging lantern lights, high ceilings). The menu at this light-filled Highland Park favorite includes shrimp wontons, mapo tofu, dan dan noo-dles, and minced pork over rice. Wash it all down with milk tea drinks made with house-made puddings and tapioca balls.

14. Kismet
4648 Hollywood Boulevard, Los Feliz

Sara Kramer and Sarah Hymanson are the chefs behind Kismet, a light, airy, all-day showcase of local produce and flavors from across the Middle East and North Africa. The menu changes frequently, but you can count on dishes like flaky malawach with sea-sonal spreads, marinated feta with olives, Moroccan-spiced carrots with cilantro and ginger, seared squid, lamb ribs, and a rotating slew of specials. The nearby Kismet Rotisserie focuses on delicious chicken with all the sides.

15. Los Cinco Puntos
3300 East Chavez Avenue, East Los Angeles
An East LA carnitas institution, Los Cinco Puntos has been turning out tacos stuffed with everything from that signature braised pork to crispy chicharrón, as well as meats by the pound, for decades. With no indoor seating, you'll have to perch on the ledge outside, or better yet, buy a bag of fluffy tortillas to go and enjoy them in the car or wherever you're staying.

16. Lupe's #2
4642 East 3rd Street, East Los Angeles
Bean-and-cheese burritos are perhaps the most famous dish in the predominantly Latino neighborhoods of Boyle Heights and East LA. Lupe's serves one

of the most-talked-about bean-and-cheese in town, laced as you wish with red or green chiles. This East LA walk-up stand, which boasts twelve types of burritos on its iconic sign, is still worth the hype.

17. Mariscos Jalisco
3040 East Olympic Boulevard, Boyle Heights
If you only visit one mariscos truck in Los Angeles, make it this one. While there is obviously no shortage of outstanding taco trucks in Los Angeles, Mariscos Jalisco may very well be the most beloved thanks to Raul Ortega and his crispy shrimp tacos. The wonderful textural interplay of the crunchy shell and shrimp filling topped with avocado-studded salsa can't be beat. And don't sleep on the aguachiles and ceviches while you're there.

18. Otomisan
2506½ 1st Street, Boyle Heights
Years ago, Boyle Heights was an enclave for Japanese immigrants. One of the few reminders of this is Otomisan, a cozy family-run restaurant with counter seating and a handful of booths to enjoy Japanese comfort-food classics and affordable sushi. After decades of business, it's still beloved by the community. Try the fantastic tonkatsu curry plate.

19. Otoño
5715 North Figueroa Street, Highland Park
Swing into this modern Highland Park spot for chef Teresa Montaño's expertly crafted Spanish menu. Sip on a well-made cocktail or some cider while nibbling on delicate ribbons of jamón Ibérico de Bellota or boquerones y mantequilla (white anchovies with butter) to start. Sharing a large pan of paella is a must; the negra version, made with squid ink, is particularly excellent.

20. Ototo
1360 Allison Avenue, Echo Park
From the same owners as ultra-popular Tsubaki (page 39), located right next door on a bustling stretch of Sunset in Echo Park, the sake situation at this always-packed mini Japanese restaurant and bar is not to be missed. Rotating little bites like karaage (Japanese fried chicken) and buta shumai (pork-and-shrimp dumplings) are meant to wet the whistle while the sake flows. Care to bring a little of the joy home? Join the sake club for three premium bottles shipped monthly.

21. Pijja Palace
2711 Sunset Boulevard,
Silver Lake

This Silver Lake sensation, which has been jam-packed since it opened in 2022, is the type of Los Angeles restaurant that defies definition. Is it a rollicking sports bar outfitted with TVs? Yes. Is it serving some of the most exciting food in town, in the form of Indian-Italian mashups like crispy bar-style pizzas topped with peri-peri vindaloo (shown above), and rigatoni tossed in creamy tomato masala? It sure is. Does it have fun cocktails and some of the best soft serve in town? Yep, it's got that too. Pijja Palace may be many things, but above all else, it's always a good time.

22. Pine & Crane
1521 Griffith Park Boulevard,
Silver Lake

The original Silver Lake location of Pine & Crane, which also has an outpost in Downtown LA, has been serving its tight menu of Taiwanese and Chinese classics since 2014. Seasonal produce is sourced from the owner's family farm, while the cooking is dependable, skilled, and fresh—making it both a neighborhood standby and a modern destination for diners who want to take a seat on a light-wood bench and dig into dan dan noodles, mapo tofu, and the like.

23. Quarter Sheets Pizza
1305 Portia Street,
Echo Park

This Echo Park darling is more than a place to nab an outstanding slice or entire pie of pan-style pizza topped with market-fresh ingredients. The wizards at this shop whip up delectable desserts, too; it's not uncommon to score a thick slice of polenta-and-olive-oil chiffon cake or an ultra-rich serving of spumoni. Add to that a dining room that feels like someone's cool basement and a good selection of natural wine, and you've got yourself a good time.

24. Rosty
5511 North Figueroa Street,
Highland Park

A casual neighborhood favorite, Highland Park's minuscule Rosty serves traditional Peruvian fare inspired by the chef's mother's restaurants in Lima. On the menu are traditional dishes like ceviche, fried rice, and lomo saltado (a dish that showcases Peruvian food's Asian and Latin influences, marrying stir-fried beef with French fries), as well as a smattering of vegetarian options.

25. Spoon & Pork
3131 West Sunset Boulevard,
Silver Lake

What humbly began as a food truck is now a chic brick-and-mortar space marked by dark gray, black, and wicker in Silver Lake. The thoughtful dishes pay homage to the comfort foods friends Raymond Yaptinchay and Jay Tuga ate while growing up in the Philippines—think sisig with Duroc pork jowl, incredibly crispy lechon kawali (deep-fried pork belly), and a unique slow-cooked fried pork shank.

26. Thunderbolt
1263 West Temple Street,
Echo Park

You're likely to find a large group of friends, people on dates, and the lone sipper all hanging out at this popular bar near Echo Park and Historic Filipinotown. Thunderbolt marries a minimalist aesthetic with a few oversized leather couches, making it an obvious choice to grab a well-made cocktail and a few equally well-made bites like pimento cheese poppers and tamari-glazed chicken drumettes.

27. Tsubaki

1356 Allison Avenue,
Echo Park

This jewel box of an izakaya in Echo Park (and attached sake bar Ototo; page 37) is known for refined Japanese cooking like dry-aged sashimi, silken tofu, and grilled meats. Don't miss the charcoal-kissed blue prawns with garlic chive butter, although any bite on the menu is going to be spectacular.

28. Valerie Echo Park

1665 Echo Park Avenue,
Echo Park

Valerie is tucked away up Echo Park Avenue, into the hills and warrens of single-family homes. As one of the only enduring businesses in that far stretch, the beloved café with covered outdoor seating has become an everyday go-to with eggs in the morning, quick-service coffee and pastries, and mellow midday meals like smoked salmon banh mi for those able to linger.

29. Villa's Tacos

5455 North Figueroa Street,
Highland Park

Villa's Tacos debuted a brick-and-mortar restaurant with a handful of outdoor picnic tables after five years of operating out of owner Victor Villa's grandmother's Highland Park house. The menu brings together family recipes with Villa's culinary flair. The signature tacos are made using blue corn tortillas with a crispy cheese-griddled interior, refried beans, onions, cilantro, crema, cotija, guacamole, and a choice of three kinds of mesquite-grilled meat.

QR CODES

for our online guides to these neighborhoods:

EASTSIDE

ECHO PARK

HIGHLAND PARK

SILVER LAKE

EASTSIDE
SHOPPING

This collection of neighborhoods east of Downtown—which includes the wide and bustling boulevards of Sunset, York, and Figueroa—has some of the most exciting shopping and dining in all of the Southland. Whether in the market for the best flour tortillas, bespoke vintage barware, or vegan deli provisions, these Eastside shopping destinations have food and drink lovers covered.

1. Bar Keeper
614 North Hoover Street,
East Hollywood
Bar Keeper in East Hollywood is a must-visit for those who love to make cocktails at home. The barware boutique's founder Joe Keeper stocks shelves with high-quality spirits and bitters made by smaller producers (he has a penchant for rye whiskey, tequila, and mezcal), vintage glasses sourced from flea markets and thrift stores, and other bar supplies and tools.

2. Besties Vegan Paradise
4882 Fountain Avenue,
East Hollywood
Situated on a highly trafficked East Hollywood corner, Besties Vegan Paradise looks and feels like a neighborhood liquor store. But scratch beneath the surface to find an incredible assortment of plant-based gas station goodies, like jerky, cookies, chips, chocolates, and even cheeses. For those who don't want to shop on an empty stomach, hot dogs and soft serve are available for on-site eating.

3. Bhan Kanom Thai
5271 Hollywood Boulevard,
East Hollywood
Tucked into one of Thai Town's busiest plazas, Bhan Kanom Thai specializes in Thai desserts and packaged snacks. The remarkable assortment of sweets goes beyond the usual mangoes with sticky rice and includes pang chi (lavender-hued griddle cakes made with taro, coconut, and corn), banana leaf–wrapped sticky rice filled with bananas or taro, pandan pudding, and more. Also find an array of packaged cookies, snacks, and candies imported from Thailand.

4. Cookbook
1549 Echo Park Avenue,
Echo Park
Every inch of this five-hundred-square-foot Echo Park greengrocer is crammed with locally grown produce, everyday staples like meat, cheese, butter, and eggs, and delicious products from LA makers. Find crusty loaves from Bub and Grandma's, small-batch tortillas from Kernel of Truth Organics, and silken tofu from Meiji. A second outlet of Cookbook is in Highland Park.

8. Le Bon Garçon

5158 Hollywood Boulevard,
Thai Town

Candymaker Justin Chao launched Le Bon Garçon more than a decade ago after studying pastry arts in Paris at the Bellouet Conseil and at two-star Michelin restaurant Le Meurice. The specialty at this curbside pickup-only location is French-style caramels that are incredibly silky and pleasingly chewy without being overly sticky—a true feat in the world of soft candies. Le Bon Garçon's suite of standby flavors includes rich and buttery salted caramels and bright and tangy mango–passion fruit caramels. Don't miss the limited-run seasonal flavors that change from month to month.

9. Maciel's Plant-Based Butcher Shop

5933 York Boulevard,
Highland Park

Visit Los Angeles's first-ever vegan butcher shop for well-constructed sand-wiches piled high with deli meats and cheeses made from scratch by chef and owner Maciel Bañales Luna. A Reuben sandwich is lay-ered with pastrami, sauer-kraut, and provolone, while Italian hoagies boast salami, pastrami, provolone, and more. The Highland Park shop also sells picnic-perfect vegan meats and cheeses packaged and ready to go.

5. El Mercadito

3425 1st Street,
Boyle Heights

For a shopping bonanza like no other, spend an afternoon at El Mercadito in Boyle Heights. The three-story shopping center, which is known to locals as El Mercadito, or "little market," is home to dozens of stalls selling everything from cowboy hats and folklorico dresses to spices and moles for home cooks and Mexican crafts and candies. Visit the top-floor, full-service restaurant or the fast-casual stalls selling churros and agua frescas to properly fuel up for a day of shopping.

6. Friends & Family

5150 Hollywood Boulevard,
East Hollywood

Roxana Jullapat bakes her heart out at Friends & Family in East Hollywood. The selection of morn-ing pastries, which are made from locally sourced heirloom grains and include morning buns, scones, croissants, and more, never ceases to amaze patrons. Don't forget to stock up on Jullapat's scratch-made granola and seasonal jams.

7. La Azteca Tortilleria

4538 East Cesar
E. Chavez Avenue,
East Los Angeles

Head to this legendary East Los Angeles tortilleria for corn and flour tortillas sold by the dozen. The difference between typical mass-produced supermar-ket tortillas and the hand-made wonders at La Azteca Tortilleria is obvious at first bite. While the former crack as they roll, the latter are impossibly plush. Get a chile relleno–stuffed burrito for the road.

10. Milkfarm
2106 Colorado Boulevard, Eagle Rock

Eagle Rock's Milkfarm is a one-stop shop for cut-to-order cheese, charcuterie, and LA-made artisanal food products. The shop's cheesemongers are second to none and always ready to introduce shoppers to something new, from lard-rubbed Spanish goat cheese to domestic soft-ripened morcella. The lunch menu changes daily with sandwiches, pastries, and cheese and charcuterie plates.

11. Sara's Market
3455 City Terrace Drive, East Los Angeles

Handed down for three generations, Sara's Market in East LA is a community hub for all that's good to eat. The corner market sells locally made staples, including wine, coffee, and tortillas, and plays host to burgeoning restaurant entrepreneurs with food trucks and food vendors setting up shop in front of the market regularly.

12. Silverlake Wine
2395 Glendale Boulevard A, Silver Lake

Stock up on wine and locally made liquor at this longtime neighborhood shop. Find bottles of Future Gin, which is distilled from Meyer lemon, honeysuckle, and grape leaves in Downtown Los Angeles, along with gin, vodka, and whiskey from Mulholland Distilling. Also for sale are bottles of Wilder Gin from nearby Ventura.

13. Wine + Eggs
3129½ Glendale Boulevard, Atwater Village

Every neighborhood needs a well-stocked and expertly curated market like Wine + Eggs in Atwater Village. In addition to pantry staples like olive oil, pasta, and whole-wheat flour, the shop carries a handful of specialty items made by local legends, including strawberry preserves from Harry's Berries, chocolates from Valerie (page 39), and peanuts with sea moss from Woon.

14. Yolk
3910 West Sunset Boulevard, Silver Lake

Those who come into Yolk seeking gifts for others often leave with something for themselves, too.
The cute and colorful selections of house and kitchen wares are as functional as they are fashionable, especially the LA-centric drinking glasses featuring various neighborhoods and freeways. They always seem to sell out fast, so snag one if any are left on the shelf.

BEYOND RESTAURANTS

Coffee Shops:
Bloom & Plume Coffee
Civil Coffee
Dinosaur Coffee
Intelligentsia Coffee
    Silver Lake Coffeebar
Kumquat Coffee
Maru Coffee

Bars:
Barcade
Bar Stella
Button Mash
Capri Club
Gold Line
Good Housekeeping
Red Lion Tavern
Tiki Ti

Bakeries:
Clark Street
La Mascota Bakery
La Monarca Bakery &
    Café
Proof Bakery

Ice Cream:
La Jerezana
Magpies Softserve
Pazzo Gelato
Scoops

STAR SIGHTINGS

Welcome to Tinseltown, where it's not unusual to see celebrities, well, everywhere, from LAX to the drugstore. Here are a handful of food and drink spots where chances are high you will recognize a famous face.

Alfred Coffee
8509 Melrose Avenue, West Hollywood
The West Hollywood location of this mini coffee chain is where you might catch actors and musicians ordering their caffeinated beverage of choice.

Casa Vega
13301 Ventura Boulevard, Sherman Oaks
Quentin Tarantino's *Once Upon a Time in Hollywood* wasn't the only time a crew of stars hit this Valley Mexican staple (page 99).

Chateau Marmont
8221 Sunset Boulevard, West Hollywood
The bungalows, restaurant, and bar at this legendary hotel on the Sunset Strip are all still a big-time celebrity draw after years of gossip, scandal, and reports of salacious behavior.

Craig's
8826 Melrose Avenue, West Hollywood
Opened by former Dan Tana's maître d' Craig Susser more than a decade ago, this swank West Hollywood hang has become a classic in its own right, serving seasonal pizzas, steaks, and its own chicken parm to bold-faced names.

Dan Tana's
9071 Santa Monica Boulevard, West Hollywood
The red booths here regularly host celebrities old and new who come for chicken parm and retro vibes (page 90).

Erewhon
Multiple locations
You'll find celebrities of all stripes getting their $20 smoothies, breakfast burritos made with organic eggs, and jars of bone broth at every location of this so-very-LA local supermarket chain.

Giorgio Baldi
114 West Channel Road, Santa Monica
A dimly lit, clubby Italian spot tucked off the Pacific Coast Highway in Santa Monica Canyon, Giorgio Baldi is where celeb cheat days happen over plates of sweet-corn agnolotti.

Mother Wolf
1545 Wilcox Avenue, Hollywood
Hollywood loves a Hollywood restaurant, and this upscale Italian spot (page 160) from Evan Funke is as luxe as they come.

Wally's
214 Wilshire Boulevard, Santa Monica
Wally's is a chichi wine bar and market where celebrities and locals alike fulfill their champagne wishes and cheese-and-charcuterie-plate dreams.

LA ESSENTIALS

By Farley Elliott

MEXICAN CUISINE

Los Angeles is a city, quite literally, built on Mexican land and heritage. Mexican families, early rancheros, Californios, and immigrants founded this city formally after thousands of years of indigenous life, and many of the city's most enduringly familiar flavors and foods still pull back to those earliest days. By some metrics, Los Angeles is the second-largest Mexican city in the world, behind only Mexico City proper, and its foodways are still undeniably tied to Mexico. Today the two countries share a formless culinary ebb and flow, with hyper-regional Mexican cuisines and dishes showing up in communities across Los Angeles County, and trends and flavors returning to Mexico by way of social media, frequent travelers, and families.

The most enduring Mexican dish in the Los Angeles lexicon has to be tamales, that masa-forward pre-Hispanic staple that is served here in restaurants, on street corners, at bus stops, and in backyards year-round. Each tamal tells a story; how it's wrapped, what it's filled with, and the way in which it's prepared and presented can all be deeply meaningful and representative.

Tamales were LA's first formalized street food, too. Early travelogues describe tamale vendors and other outdoor food setups at length. Served hot, the highly portable tamal (shown at left) made for an ideal start to the day and a late-evening soak-up after a night of heavy drinking—and the same is true today. Tamale vendors still make up a sizable chunk of the city's ten thousand–plus street food operators, with many selling out of simple coolers near transit points for commuters to enjoy. Most Mexican corner bakeries will also sell tamales, especially as Christmas and cooler weather creep up. For best-in-class tamales, consider the historic Mexican bakery **La Flor de Yucatán** (page 136) in the Pico-Union neighborhood just west of Downtown or the staple corner restaurant **Los Cinco Puntos** (page 37) at the edge of Boyle Heights and East LA.

If the tamale vendor represents the historic beating heart of Los Angeles street food, it is the ubiquitous taquero who is the movement's face. On any given night in greater LA, hundreds of taco vendors set up on sidewalks, along old railroad tracks, and in car wash parking lots to sell tacos. The quality and style vary wildly from stand to stand, and that's part of the fun. Every Angeleno worth their salt has at least one taco spot in their back pocket at all times, the place that is guaranteed to satisfy when the need arises.

There are LA-beloved taco trucks like **Mariscos Jalisco** (page 37), selling diced, spiced, and fried shrimp tacos. There are Netflix-famous restaurants like **Sonoratown** (page 71), where fans line up down the block for handmade flour tortillas and smoky mesquite-kissed carne asada. And there are everyday stands that sell under a simple string of lights on sidewalks across the city. They are often unnamed and have no social media presence; their only goal is to feed the people where they're at, usually at a price point that ensures access for all.

Beyond tacos and tortillas, Los Angeles remains a land where regional variety is limitless. Mexican states from Michoacán to Oaxaca to Puebla and far beyond find purchase here, with home cooks, restaurants, and pop-ups selling deeply personal foods to those in the know. In recent years, Northern Mexico–style flour tortilla spots have emerged selling fire-grilled meats with lots of mashed avocado and fiery salsas, like at the roving **El Ruso** (page 136) truck. Oaxacan food has always had more than a foothold here, with moles and tlayudas—a Oaxacan specialty comprised of a large tortilla that's slathered with refried beans and other toppings, then grilled—and stews and snacks sold at restaurants along LA's Westside and in Koreatown, particularly at **Gish Bac** (page 136) and the long-running **Guelaguetza Restaurant** (page 103). The city's love of stewed birria (often beef today, but also goat) has become so pervasive—find it at spots like **Birrieria Gonzalez** in East LA and **El Parian** in Pico-Union—that the specialty from the Jalisco region has moved back south of the border in recent years, with cheese-crusted fried quesabirria tacos emerging as a new street favorite in places like Tijuana, where it wasn't traditionally found as readily.

In formal restaurants, a new kind of Mexican and

Mexican American cooking has also emerged in recent years. Traditional ingredients, pre-Hispanic dishes, and LA's love of big, often spicy flavors have merged to make a modern Mexican movement here feel vital. **Damian** (page 67), the first Los Angeles restaurant from chef Enrique Olvera, has become a staple in the ultra-hip Arts District, while chefs like Thomas Ortega of **Playa Amor** and Carlos Salgado of Orange County's **Taco Maria** continue to push the modern California-Mexican food scene in new directions. It's just as easy today to find bold Mexican and Mexican American flavors fused with Texas barbecue (at **Moo's Craft Barbecue**, page 139, in Lincoln Heights, or **Heritage Barbecue** in Oceanside) as it was to find tamale vendors on the street 150 years ago.

Birrieria Gonzalez
Multiple locations

El Parian
1528 West Pico Boulevard, Downtown

Playa Amor
6527 Pacific Coast Highway, Long Beach

Heritage Barbecue
2002 South Coast Highway, Oceanside

STREET FOOD

More than a century and a half on, Los Angeles remains the street-food epicenter of America. The city hosts tens of thousands of vendors on its streets, from hot dog sellers outside stadiums and concerts to blocks-long stalls selling all manner of Thai street snacks. Everyone eats at street-food stands in Los Angeles—and often, that's where some of the city's best food can be found.

Despite the region's millions of annual tourists and the city's own attempts to highlight street vending as a public good—particularly in poorer communities that may also be food deserts—most non-Angelenos are shocked to learn that the vast majority of street vendors still operate without a license. Travelers today can easily spot a taco stand, wood-fired pizza trailer, or street noodle vendor selling right on the sidewalk; what's harder to see are the complex laws and confusing red tape that continue to hinder LA's vendors from easily reaching full legalization.

While tacos, tamales, and hot dogs are ubiquitous around Los Angeles, they are certainly not the only available street-food options. Today's ever-morphing street scene caters to seemingly every cuisine, dish, and price point there is. At the **Wat Thai** temple in North Hollywood, more than a dozen long-running vendors sell noodles, meat skewers, and sugary snacks from a parking lot, while the weekend **Alameda Night Market** in Downtown LA hosts a rotating collection of vendors that can range from birria ramen makers and cake bite dessert stands to teriyaki rice bowl specialists. Pass by on the right night on **York Boulevard** in Highland Park and find more than a dozen stands selling vegan food, hand-pulled noodles, and Neapolitan-style pizzas. Want Filipino meat skewers that you grill yourself instead? Try **Dollar Hits** in Historic Filipinotown. Need a cheese-crusted breakfast burrito? Seek out **Lowkey Burritos** on Instagram.

Much of the modern street food scene—particularly when it comes to the wide variety of colorful food trucks—is thanks to Roy Choi, who earned nationwide acclaim with his fleet of **Kogi** (page 105) rigs, selling Korean-Mexican mash-up dishes.

Kogi's rise coincided with the early days of Twitter, when the novelty of seeking out roving underground vendors was at its peak. Today, because there are so many street sellers in seemingly every neighborhood, teppanyaki trucks, Philly cheesesteak operators, and other mobile vendors are more likely to cluster together at office parks and one-off food festivals.

Los Angeles is also a premier burger town (more on that later), and on any given night it's possible to find smash burger specialists griddling up beef outside of dive bars, breweries, and wine bars all over the city. But for the most bang-for-buck flavor, it's best to hit a pop-up market like **Mercado Olympic**, just east of Downtown's core, where unique regional Mexican delights are plentiful. On Sundays, **Smorgasburg** (page 155) plays host to dozens of unique vendors selling everything from boba and barbecue to shrimp bowls carved out of pineapples, and seasonal events like **KTown Night Market** and **626 Night Market** offer a slew of pan-Asian stands selling desserts, meats, dumplings, and beyond.

Alameda Night Market
1123 South Main Street, Downtown

Dollar Hits
2432 West Temple Street, Historic Filipinotown

CALIFORNIA CUISINE

If Mexican food and street food (and fast food, but more on that in a moment) are staples of the everyday Angeleno diet, then the broad, nebulous "California cuisine" is what people outside of LA *think* that Angelenos eat. Barely dressed salads, avocado toast, and expensive adaptogen smoothies are hallmarks of any quick joke about LA eaters—often punctuated further by references to yoga pants and social media influencer lifestyles. And the truth is, there is some honesty in the sentiment, though LA's culinary reality is obviously much more dynamic. The often organic-leaning, vegetable-forward, vegan-friendly California restaurant today is just as likely to serve falafel or house-made pasta as it is to put fermented fruits in a grain bowl or a soft-boiled egg inside of an arugula-heavy breakfast sandwich served on local bread from **Bub and Grandma's**.

The root of California cuisine dates back nearly fifty years to restaurants like Berkeley's Chez Panisse or Santa Monica stalwart **Michael's** (page 102), which opened in 1979. Those restaurants prioritized a triangle of then-innovative ideas: simplicity, seasonality, and local sustainability. Why fly in white asparagus from Europe or uni from Japan, the thinking went, when California's farms and fisheries already supply the nation with so much bountiful food? Why cook French food or imperial Chinese dishes exclusively when the closest we can actually get to the height of flavor is a moment spent with a perfectly ripe piece of fruit? Heady stuff, sure, but that thinking a generation ago has since helped to pave the way for so much of what Angelenos (and the rest of America) eat today. If you've recently sat down for dinner at a neighborhood small-plates restaurant with a pan-cultural menu that serves seasonal vegetables and natural wine, you have California to thank.

The buy-in from diners in those early days didn't take long. Wolfgang Puck became a household name with **Spago** (page 115) in 1982, the ultimate see-and-be-seen restaurant for fame-chasing eaters, celebrities like Jack Nicholson, and countless millionaires and billionaires. Puck's unique pizza creations (like smoked salmon) have since spawned numerous imitators and the entire California Pizza Kitchen chain, and Puck's face can now be found on television and in grocery store aisles globally. The now-closed Campanile sent the movement into overdrive when it opened in 1989, helping to solidify Nancy Silverton (who founded La Brea Bakery in the same building) as a defining force for LA food; her **Mozza** (page 104) restaurant empire today is still one of the city's best lenses through which to view California cuisine. Today **République** (page 92) occupies the former Campanile building, and

between its bustling brunch and dinner services daily it's possible to see just how far the scene has come. On any given day, a meal at République chef-owners Walter and Margarita Manzke's restaurant could include a pupusa, a Filipino rice bowl, a burger, a salad, and a plate of French pastries.

Today California cuisine is as common to Los Angeles as tacos. Hints of the flavors and format can be found up and down the economic scale, from the coast to the Inland Empire and inland Orange County. Restaurants like Santa Monica's **Rustic Canyon** (page 150) and West Hollywood's **A.O.C.** (page 89) are as likely to serve citrus salad and curried cauliflower as a hanger steak or roast chicken, while places like **Kismet** (page 36) and Silver Lake's **Botanica** (page 35) marry California abundance with light, fresh Middle Eastern flavors. For an all-day peek at California's endless brunch culture, try **Kitchen Mouse** in Highland Park or **Yang's Kitchen** (page 15) in the San Gabriel Valley, where Taiwanese and Chinese flavors speak to a modern Angeleno audience.

Bub and Grandma's
3507 Eagle Rock Boulevard, Glassell Park

Kitchen Mouse
5904 North Figueroa Street, Highland Park

FAST FOOD

If nothing else, Los Angeles's mark on the global dining scene is secure thanks to fast food, the eat-in-your-car dining experience that was created, popularized, and modernized right here in Southern California. Countless chains, from Sizzler to Taco Bell to McDonald's, were created in greater Los Angeles, and many still call the region home. But while Los Angeles hasn't exactly moved on from Panda Express (founded in 1983 inside a Glendale mall), the city has found ways to innovate the fast-food service model and basic menu to create something entirely unique to Southern California.

Locally owned "fast-food diners," for lack of a better term, can be found in every neighborhood in the city, and Angelenos know which ones they prefer. These restaurants often sport fast-food-style drive-thrus and sell everything from burgers with shredded lettuce to breakfast burritos, taco plates, gyros, and boxes of loaded, cheesy French fries. Some, like **Lucky Boy** (page 13) in Pasadena, are famous simply for their overclocked breakfast burritos. Others, like **Dino's Famous Chicken** on Pico Boulevard, have become unique destinations selling blistery grilled chicken with lots of spicy marinade over plates of fries (shown at left). There are countless knockoffs and derivatives of the original chili cheeseburger specialist **Tommy's** (page 139), too, and they usually sport increasingly unhinged names like Tomy's (one M), Tam's, and Tom's #5. Many are open from early morning to late at night, offering something for everyone, every day. And if at any time, you don't feel like ordering your "usual," LA also has drive-thru restaurants selling vegan food, tamales, fresh donuts, ramen, and beyond.

The biggest thing LA has given the world in the fast-food genre, though, has to be the cheeseburger (one prominent piece of local folklore claims that the dish was created in Pasadena). Historic and regionally specific burger restaurants have anchored the area's dining scene since the 1940s (like the sweet hickory burger at **The Apple Pan**—page 113), and today it's possible to enjoy a thin-cut pastrami-topped burger just about anywhere in the city at a moment's notice. Burgers are so ingrained in everyday LA life, in fact, that there are now dozens, if not hundreds, of burger pop-ups and street stands that sell beef-and-bun combinations every weekend. Koreatown's **Love Hour** and the roving **Yellow Paper Burger** (page 139) are stars in the smash burger world. Many original pop-up burger setups have since gone legit, like the former backyard hit **Burgers Never Say Die** in Silver Lake, and award-winning **Goldburger** (page 36) in Highland Park.

Dino's Famous Chicken
2575 West Pico Boulevard, Pico Union

Love Hour
532 South Western Avenue, Koreatown

Burgers Never Say Die
2388 Glendale Boulevard, Silver Lake

KOREAN CUISINE

In suburban LA, the pastrami burgers and chorizo tacos come easy. But for a delicious, occasionally confusing, endlessly impressive night out, it's all about Koreatown, right in the middle of the city. Koreatown is inarguably LA's most compact and vibrant dining scene, with endless restaurants settled atop and against one another in strip malls and storefronts from (loosely) Western to

Vermont. There are late-night bars, twenty-four-hour places to find tteokbokki (rice cakes), and short ribs with blow-torched cheese on top, and countless mandu (dumpling) shops, soup spots, and Korean barbecue specialists in between. In many ways the neighborhood represents Korean cuisine itself in its ingenuity.

There are more Korean nationals and Korean Americans living in greater Los Angeles than anywhere else in America—or in the world, outside the Korean peninsula. The best way to experience the culture's dining scene in one compact day is to spend time strolling Sixth Street in Koreatown, home to some of the area's most popular restaurants. Some would argue that legendary **Parks BBQ** (page 69) is the undisputed champ of high-volume, high-quality Korean barbecue, while others might hand the title to **Baekjeong** (with outlets across LA as well as New York, the Bay Area, and greater Seattle), given its endlessly long weekend lines and impossibly fast turnover. Across the street, **Sun Nong Dan** (page 71) draws its own crowds thanks to its specialty, a massive stone bowl filled with rice cakes and short ribs, served all day—while a homier, more grandmotherly stewed short rib is available at **Seong Buk Dong** (page 70) just up the street. For an eye-opening look at a more modern Korean restaurant, walk up the street to **Kinn** instead, and then finish the night at **Dan Sung Sa** (page 82), where the servers dress in army fatigues, the wood walls are carved and marred from years of friendly abuse, and the cheese corn and soju land fast at every table.

Soban (page 71), on Olympic, is a comforting staple known for its banchan and raw crab; there is **Myung In Dumplings** for Korean mandu of all sorts; and on Wilshire the place to be at three A.M. on weekends is **BCD Tofu House** (page 103), where scalding bowls of softened tofu soups with kimchi arrive to each table ready to do battle with the night's drinks. Large pockets of Korean restaurants and bars can also be found in south Los Angeles County and around Irvine in Orange County, meaning the nearest kimchi pancake is never far away.

Speaking of drinking, no mention of LA's Korean food scene would be complete without at least a passing nod to the area's many karaoke bars, where many a friend group has whiled away an evening jamming to BTS hits or eighties power ballads. **Break Room 86** is a quality option for big club-style fun in a hip and crowded space, but for individual rooms for groups and quality food and drink, it's all about **Rosen Karaoke by Pharaoh** on Eighth Street. Not feeling a night with friends over a karaoke mic? Score drinks instead at red-booth classic **the Prince** (page 70), also home to some of the city's best Korean fried chicken), dive bar classic **HMS Bounty**, or the upscale **Normandie Club** on Sixth Street.

Baekjeong
3465 West 6th Street, Koreatown

Myung In Dumplings
3109 West Olympic Boulevard, Koreatown

Break Room 86
630 South Ardmore Avenue, Koretown

Rosen Karaoke by Pharaoh
3488 West 8th Street, Koreatown

HMS Bounty
3357 Wilshire Boulevard, Koreatown

The Normandie Club
3612 West 6th Street, Koreatown

CHINESE AND TAIWANESE CUISINE

Well east of Downtown, LA's winding San Gabriel Valley is the regional epicenter for Chinese and Taiwanese cooking of all stripes. Across some three dozen neighborhoods and stand-alone cities, there are hundreds of dumpling takeouts, noodle shops, and hot-pot restaurants (to name just a few genres) all competing for business, buoyed by more than one and a half million residents with high expectations for quality, specificity, and often affordability. Asian Americans make up at least one-third of the SGV's total population, including hundreds of thousands of foreign-born Taiwanese and Chinese immigrants—a discerning audience when it comes to Chinese cuisine. International brands like the massively famous **Din Tai Fung** (page 12) or Beijing hot pot proliferator **Shancheng Lameizi**, seeking to make inroads into the American market, often must first conquer the San Gabriel Valley.

The SGV food scene is so large and diverse, it can be overwhelming even to native Angelenos. The late food critic Jonathan Gold once chronicled some two dozen regional cuisines of China across the various neighborhoods, with each independent cuisine often having dozens of restaurants within its purview. It's best, then, to try to approach LA's Chinese food scene in pieces, either regionally (by focusing in on one area like the cities of San Gabriel, Alhambra, or Temple City) or by food type. Want some of that numbing spice found most famously in Sichuan cuisine? Try the Sichuan chicken stir-fry at **Xiang La Hui** in Alhambra, the cumin toothpick lamb at **Chengdu Taste**'s multiple locations (page 11), or the tea-smoked ribs, mapo tofu, or dan dan noodles at **Sichuan Impression** (page 14). For dumpling dominance it's all about **Mama Lu's**, where dumplings are not only the staple item for on-site dining, but also available in giant frozen take-out bags for at-home eating. There's also the long, flat **Hui Tou Xiang** dumpling variety found in San Gabriel, the thick but airy Shanghai specialty sheng jian bao from **Kang Kang Shau May** in the City of Industry, and the crispy pan-fried pork dumpling style famous at **One One Dumpling**.

Banquet-style dining is also in high demand across LA's Chinese restaurant scene, particularly when it comes to big, airy dim sum dining rooms. Rosemead's **Sea Harbour** (page 104) is considered by some to be the gold standard for LA dim sum, though the newer **Bistro 1968** is the more modern darling. **Atlantic Seafood and Dim Sum** is ideal for those seeking big tables and pushcarts, while **Lunasia Dimsum House** is a great neighborhood option with multiple locations. In the evening, it's best instead to head to big, bold restaurants like **Newport Seafood Restaurant** (page 13) or **Longo Seafood** for high-end lobster, or to the Michelin-rated **Bistro Na's** (page 11) in Temple City, home of Imperial Chinese cuisine.

That's not to say that all of LA's Chinese restaurants are found in the San Gabriel Valley; only that the area represents the beating heart of Chinese dining right now. The city's historic Chinatown is also filled with favorites like **Yang Chow** (page 71—get the signature slippery shrimp) and **Qin West Noodle** at Far East Plaza, as well as old banquet dining halls and tea shops. Around the corner, **Pearl River Deli** has earned raves for its compact menu that nods to Cantonese cooking, so expect Macau-style pork chop buns, fatty pork char siu, chow fun, and more, while Downtown's **RiceBox** (page 70) leans almost exclusively into Cantonese barbecue. Farther afield, Chengdu Taste offshoot **Mian** has found a home in the West Adams neighborhood, serving spicy dan dan noodles and wontons, while **Meizhou Dongpo** in Century City wows crowds with its whole duck preparations. Mar Vista's **Little Fatty** is one of the most requested delivery and take-out restaurants in all of Los Angeles, while Highland Park's **Joy** (page 36) and sister project **Pine & Crane** (page 38) in Silver Lake and Downtown serve beef rolls, mapo tofu, minced pork over rice, and other staple Taiwanese dishes to leagues of adoring fans daily.

Shancheng Lameizi
1530 South San Gabriel Boulevard, San Gabriel

Xiang La Hui
621 West Main Street, Alhambra

Mama Lu's Dumpling House
700 North Spring Street, Chinatown

Hui Tou Xiang
1643 North Cahuenga Boulevard, West Hollywood

Kang Kang Shau May
18017 Gale Avenue, City of Industry

One One Dumpling
704 West Las Tunas Drive, San Gabriel

Bistro 1968
402 South San Gabriel Boulevard,
San Gabriel

Atlantic Seafood and Dim Sum
500 North Atlantic Boulevard, Monterey Park

Lunasia Dimsum House
Multiple locations

Longo Seafood
7540 Garvey Avenue, Rosemead

Qin West Noodle
Multiple locations

Pearl River Deli
935 Mei Ling Way, Chinatown

Mian
5263 West Adams Boulevard, West Adams

Meizhou Dongpo
10250 Santa Monica Boulevard, Century City

Little Fatty
3809 Grand View Boulevard, Mar Vista

LA'S MANY OTHER ASIAN CUISINES

A whole anthology of guidebooks could be written about LA's additional Asian cuisines, each of which offers its own neighborhood (or city) rich with restaurants serving regional delights. Suffice it to say that there is simply not enough room here, unfortunately, to give them all the justice, so consider what follows to be a very introductory primer on where to go and what to eat.

While greater Southern California's epicenter for Vietnamese dining is most certainly just over the LA border in the Orange County city of Westminster (go eat at **Brodard**, seriously), great Vietnamese food is actually pretty widely available across the region. Pho is in long supply everywhere, including at staple **Pho 79** and the delightfully punny **Phorage** in West LA; for crispy egg rolls it's all about **Golden Deli** (page 12); for banh mi it's hard to beat **Hue Thai Bakery & Deli** and **Ba Le**, both in the San Gabriel Valley. Silver Lake's **Bé Ù** does street snacks, and for modern interpretations of Vietnamese flavors, try **Cassia** (page 145) in Santa Monica.

Greater LA's Thai food scene is also more than generous, with a whole corner of the East Hollywood neighborhood operating as Thai Town, a hub for boat noodles, meat skewers, crab with garlic, and beyond. **Jitlada** (page 102) is the spicy-as-heck local favorite, and with nearly four hundred menu items, it could take a lifetime to work through everything here. **Northern Thai Food Club** has become the hot new kid on the block, while **Luv2eat Thai Bistro** (page 90) farther west on Sunset is a must for noodle soups, yellow curry, and sticky rice. **Ruen Pair** is the late-night place for after-hours eating and one seriously spicy papaya salad, while **Sapp Coffee Shop** remains a cash-only strip-mall staple serving boat noodles and jade noodles. Want more of an experience? Get to North Hollywood's **Wat Thai** temple for its weekend street food bazaar, try **Anajak Thai**'s Taco Tuesday night alleyway parties, or step into the colorful candy wonderland that is **Bhan Kanom Thai** (page 40) on Hollywood Boulevard.

For decades LA's South Bay region has been home to all manner of Japanese restaurants, thanks largely to the emergence of Japan's automotive industry in the United States. With stateside headquarters based in and around Torrance, Toyota and Honda and others also imported a need for delicious Japanese food at all prices. Today the area is rich with restaurants, from izakaya **Otafuku** (page 129) in Gardena to soba specialist **Ichimiann** (page 129). Farther north there's Sawtelle Japantown for the Westsiders, a neighborhood packed with ramen spots (**Tsujita LA Artisan Noodle**, page 116, is the undisputed king), snack shops, and locally made sake thanks to Sawtelle Sake. Eastsiders have Little Tokyo in Downtown and its many restaurants and shops, from **Daikokuya** for ramen to neighbor **Marugame Monzo** for udon. **Izakaya Bizan** offers a variety of flame-grilled meats, and **Fugetsu-Do** (page 73) is

the place to find LA's oldest mochi. For a more modern look at Japanese eating, try the many sushi restaurants of the San Fernando Valley (**Shin Sushi** in Encino—page 135—or **Asanebo** in Studio City, in particular) or the sake-and-snacks combo at Echo Park's **Ototo** (page 37). And, of course, no visit to Los Angeles would be complete without the excellent sushi (page 134) that's served everywhere from tiny spots in strip malls to the ubiquitous and massively popular local chain **Sugarfish** to extremely precise (and pricey) omakase spots.

While LA's Chinese and Korean cuisines certainly deserve their fair share of love, it has been heartening more recently to see Filipino food earn more time in the spotlight. Los Angeles has a massive Filipino population, long centered around Historic Filipinotown just outside of Downtown, and today the scene has expanded to nearly every neighborhood in the city. For grill-your-own meat skewers get to **Dollar Hits**, and for comforting family classics try **Kusina Filipina** in Eagle Rock. Downtown's **Sari Sari Store** at Grand Central Market (page 67) attracts workers, tourists, and everyone else, while Filipinotown barbecue spot **The Park's Finest** is the hands-down spot for smoky mash-ups like coconut beef adobo and bibingka corn bread. **Kuya Lord** is among the best of the newer bunch, serving lechon and noodles and lovingly grilled shrimp on Melrose, while **Lasita** (page 68) in Chinatown is the hotspot dinner destination for natural wine and big Filipino flavors.

In Long Beach, at the southern coastal end of the county, Cambodian food is the order of the day. The city's large Cambodian population immigrated decades ago and has woven itself into the fabric of everyday dining there, from spots like the staple noodle and porridge restaurant **Phnom Penh Noodle Shack** to **Kim Sun Kitchen** (for beef noodle soup) to **A&J Seafood Shack**, where garlic shrimp, lobster plates, and spring rolls require special attention. Don't forget the region's many Cambodian-founded donut shops, either.

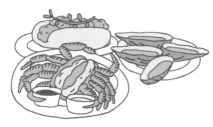

Brodard
16105 Brookhurst Street, Westminster

Pho 79
9941 Hazard Avenue, Garden Grove

Phorage
3300 Overland Avenue, West LA

Hue Thai Bakery & Deli
8968 Garvey Avenue, Rosemead

Ba Le
1426 South Atlantic Boulevard, Alhambra

Bé Ù
557 North Hoover Street, Silver Lake

Northern Thai Food Club
5301 Sunset Boulevard, Thai Town

Ruen Pair
5257 Hollywood Boulevard, Thai Town

Sapp Coffee Shop
5183 Hollywood Boulevard, Thai Town

Anajak Thai
14704 Ventura Boulevard, Sherman Oaks

Daikokuya
327 1st Street, Little Tokyo

Marugame Monzo
329 1st Street, Little Tokyo

Izakaya Bizan
333 South Alameda Street #314, Little Tokyo

Asanebo
11941 Ventura Boulevard, Studio City

Dollar Hits
2432 West Temple Street, Historic Filipinotown

Kusina Filipina
4157 Eagle Rock Boulevard, Eagle Rock

The Park's Finest
1267 West Temple Street, Historic Filipinotown

Kuya Lord
5003 Melrose Avenue, Hollywood

Phnom Penh Noodle Shack
1644 Cherry Avenue, Long Beach

Kim Sun Kitchen
5449 Cherry Avenue, Long Beach

A&J Seafood Shack
3201 East Anaheim Street, Long Beach

PAN–MIDDLE EASTERN CUISINES

Proper attention must be paid to the large Persian and Armenian communities of Los Angeles as well. These are groups with long histories in the region. In Glendale, just north of Downtown, tens of thousands of Armenians have come to define an entire dining scene, with restaurants serving sit-down feasts, grab-and-go kabob plates, Georgian and Russian offshoot dishes, and everything else in between. **Carousel** and **Elena's** are key for big group feasts of rice, meat, and roasted vegetables (as is **Marouch** in East Hollywood), while **Monta Factory** is the spot for tiny take-out dumplings eaten en masse at home. Glendale's best overall Armenian restaurant has to be **Mini Kabob**, tucked away on a side street—just don't expect sit-down service from this family-run spot known for its big platters of lamb chops, lule (minced lamb kebabs), and ikra (a smoky dip made with twice-cooked eggplant). And for delicious and unique eats in Glendale, get to **Zhengyalov Hatz**

for the simple, herby flatbread wraps made to order (shown to the left), or **Khinkali House** for Georgian-Armenian fare, including big, juicy, knobby dumplings the size of a fist.

Head west to find the culinary heart of LA's Persian diaspora, a place known as Tehrangeles near Westwood and the 405. Here a slew of Iranian delights are available, including soup and sandwiches at the day-time-only classic **Attari** (page 117), or a plate of kabobs and koobideh from the always crowded **Taste of Tehran** (page 115). Over on Santa Monica Boulevard, **Darya Restaurant** is the place for large parties (for Eastsiders, **Raffi's Place** and **Pardis** fit the bill), and don't forget to finish strong with some specialty Persian ice cream from **Saffron & Rose**.

LA's Israeli cuisine has also caught on more broadly, moving from its hub in the San Fernando Valley—affectionately known as the Kosher Corridor—into more mainstream pan–Middle Eastern restaurants like **Bavel** (page 67) in the Arts District and **Saffy's** in East Hollywood. **Ta-eem Grill** on Melrose is a boisterous spot for sandwiches and plates of shawarma (all kosher), while the local chain **Mizlala** (page 129) does fast Israeli small plates to perfection. Back in the Valley, **Tel Aviv Fish Grill** is a spot for tender seafood, Tarzana's **Hummus Bar & Grill** is famous for its Jerusalem mix of chicken parts, liver, and more, and the single busiest place of all has to be **Borekas**, a take-out-only pastry operation that plays to insanely long lines.

Carousel
5112 Hollywood Boulevard #107, Thai Town

Elena's
1000 South Glendale Avenue, Glendale

Marouch
4905 Santa Monica Boulevard, East Hollywood

Monta Factory
1208 West Glenoaks Boulevard, Glendale

Mini Kabob
313 1/2 Vine Street, Glendale

Zhengyalov Hatz
318 East Broadway, Glendale

Khinkali House
113 Artsakh Avenue, Glendale

Darya Restaurant
12130 Santa Monica Boulevard, West LA

Raffi's Place
211 East Broadway, Glendale

Pardis
738 North Glendale Avenue, Glendale

Saffron & Rose
387 Westwood Boulevard, Westwood

Saffy's
4845 Fountain Avenue, East Hollywood

Ta-eem Grill
7422 Melrose Avenue, Hollywood

Tel Aviv Fish Grill
19014 Ventura Boulevard, Tarzana

Hummus Bar & Grill
18743 Ventura Boulevard, Tarzana

Borekas Sephardic Pastries
15030 Ventura Boulevard, Sherman Oaks

LA FOOD GLOSSARY

By Matthew Kang and Cathy Chaplin

Açaí bowl: One of LA's popular breakfast options is actually a Brazilian dessert of blended açaí berries topped with fresh fruit. The company Sambazon was the first to import frozen açai to the US in the early 2000s, launching in LA before expanding to other cities. These days, açaí bowls can be found across the city, often incorporating toppings like granola, berries, and nuts.

Al pastor: This style of spit-grilled pork originated in Mexico City or Puebla. The pork is typically marinated with pineapple, chiles, and spices, and served in tacos along with chopped onion, cilantro, and sometimes chopped pineapple.

Angeleno: This term refers to a native Los Angeles resident or a long-time transplant.

Birria: Originally from Jalisco, Mexico, this specialty of oven-roasted, adobo-rubbed goat or lamb served with consommé made from pan drippings is traditionally served at breakfast. The versions found in LA range from Jalisco-style, oven-roasted goat birria to Tijuana-style, boiled beef (birria de res). The former is served with consommé, tortillas, and garnishes for DIY tacos, while the latter comes ready-made into tacos and a cup of consommé. Lately LA has been seeing more quesatacos (birria tacos with the addition of melted cheese), a phenomenon from Tijuana that became popular around 2016, when a number of vendors, perhaps most notably Teddy's Red Tacos, started promoting them on Instagram.

Boba: Boba are sweet and chewy tapioca balls usually served with chilled milk tea and an extra-wide straw. Los Angeles is the epicenter of boba culture in the US due to a vast Asian American population, with the San Gabriel Valley boasting the most boba shops per capita in the country.

Carne asada: LA's most popular taco style originated in Tijuana and Sinaloa and consists of marinated beef, ideally grilled over charcoal, though you'll also find it cooked on a gas or flat-top grill.

Carnitas: This traditional dish of slowly braised or simmered pork hails from the western Mexican state of Michoacán, and is typically made with pork shoulder due to its rich marbling. The pork is usually covered in lard to make it easy to shred post-cooking, and comes served simply with tortillas or in tacos, burritos, and the like.

The Eastside: The Eastside is an official region that includes East Los Angeles, Boyle Heights, Lincoln Heights, and El Sereno. Not to be confused with the eastside (note: lowercase "e"), which can include all neighborhoods east of Downtown.

French dip: This meat-filled sandwich (roast beef, roast pork, leg of lamb, turkey, pastrami, or ham) is served on crusty bread with a side of jus. It was purportedly invented at Philippe The Original in Chinatown (page 69), but also claimed by Cole's (page 83) in Downtown.

Hot pot: This communal dish consisting of flavored broth simmered atop a portable heat source is served alongside various proteins and vegetables for cooking in the bubbling stock. Though originally from China, hot pot is also popular at Taiwanese and Japanese restaurants. Individual-size hot pots, along with condiment bars, have grown in popularity in Los Angeles in recent years.

Korean barbecue: Thinly sliced meats, including beef, pork, and chicken, but also duck, seafood, and lamb, are typically cooked by diners on a tabletop grill and served with a variety of banchan (palate-cleansing snacks). From premium barbecue spots to reasonably priced all-you-can-eat places, there are a variety of barbecuing options in Koreatown.

Pupusa: Pupusas are Salvadoran cornmeal griddle cakes filled simply with cheese or more elaborately with meats and even loroco blossoms.

SGV or 626: These terms are short-hand for the San Gabriel Valley, an area east of Downtown Los Angeles that spans almost three hundred square miles.

Shawarma: Shawarma refers to the spit-roasted, thinly shaved meats (from chicken to lamb and beef and beyond) that abound in Los Angeles thanks to the city's thriving Armenian, Lebanese, Israeli, and Arabic populations. Head to the San Fernando Valley or pockets of Glendale and East Hollywood for this satisfying specialty.

The Southland: This term is shorthand for the massive metropolitan region in and around greater Los Angeles, including the Inland Empire and Orange County.

Street dogs: A local take on Mexican hot dogs, these bacon-wrapped franks are topped with griddled onions, bell peppers, and jalapeños, then garnished with ketchup, mayonnaise, and mustard. Vendors selling street dogs emerge across the city starting at sundown, especially around popular concert venues like the Hollywood Bowl, Wiltern, or Palladium.

Tlayuda: A thin, wide tortilla is slathered with asiento (unrefined lard), beans, cabbage, salsa, avocado, and wisps of Oaxacan cheese, then grilled over charcoal or gas to make a tlayuda. Meats can also be added on top, such as tasajo (dried beef), moronga (blood sausage), chorizo, or cecina (thin, salted meat).

The Valley: This is shorthand for the San Fernando Valley, a vast region located north of the Los Angeles Basin spanning more than two hundred square miles and divided into thirty-four neighborhoods, including Sherman Oaks, Studio City, Burbank, and Glendale.

The Westside: Often used colloquially to describe any neighborhood west of the 405 freeway, the Westside is an official region that includes twenty-three neighborhoods, stretching from Pacific Palisades to Marina del Rey to the west and Beverly Crest to Ladera Heights to the east.

Arts District
Chinatown
Downtown
Koreatown
Little Tokyo

DOWN
& KORE

3

TOWN
ATOWN

DOWNTOWN & KOREATOWN

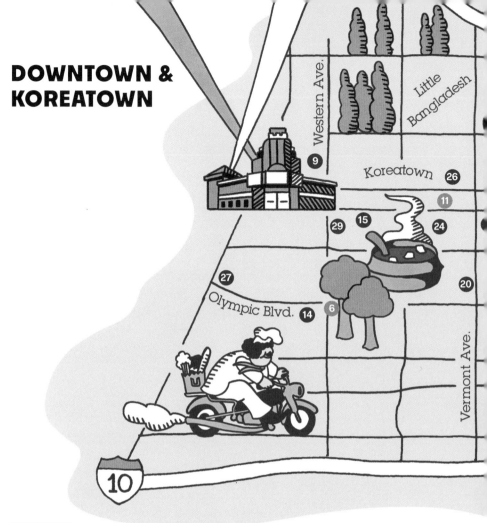

DINING

1. Badmaash
2. Bar Amá
3. Bavel
4. Bestia
5. Camphor
6. Damian
7. Danny Boy's Famous Original Pizza
8. Grand Central Market
9. Han Bat Seol Lung Tang
10. Kato Restaurant
11. Kobawoo House
12. Lasita
13. Manuela
14. Mapo Dak Galbi
15. MDK Noodles (Myung Dong Kyoja)
16. Mexicali Taco & Co.
17. My Dung Sandwich Shop
18. Nick's Cafe
19. Otium
20. Parks BBQ
21. Philippe The Original
22. Pho 87
23. Pizzeria Bianco
24. The Prince
25. RiceBox
26. Seong Buk Dong
27. Soban
28. Sonoratown
29. Sun Nong Dan
30. Yang Chow

SHOPPING

1. Anzen Hardware
2. Artbook @ Hauser & Wirth
3. Chado Tea Room
4. Fugetsu-Do
5. Greenbar Distillery
6. Koreatown Galleria
7. LAX-C
8. The Library Store
9. Now Serving
10. Olvera Street
11. Open Market
12. Phoenix Bakery
13. Row DTLA
14. Utsuwa-No-Yakata

DOWNTOWN & KOREATOWN
DINING

Each and every neighborhood within this broad swath of land that we're loosely defining as Downtown and Koreatown is so packed with places to eat, it could easily warrant its own chapter. You have the historic heart of Downtown, where you'll find the Broad museum, the Walt Disney Concert Hall, LA Live, and Crypto.com Arena (formerly Staples Center), the home of the Lakers and Clippers. Dining-wise, the area has a little bit of everything—from sought-after tasting menus to rooftop hotel bars with great views to restaurants serving Cantonese roast pork hiding inside office buildings. On the eastern edge of Downtown and flanked by the Los Angeles River, there's the Arts District, once an urban industrial zone that in recent years has developed into one of the most vibrant neighborhoods in the city, thanks to the energy Bestia brought to the area when it opened in 2012 (more on that on page 67). The restaurants here are big, beautiful, and bustling. Nearby Chinatown bursts with essential and long-standing restaurants that merit a visit, as well as more modern gems that have brought a newfound sense of vibrancy to the area.

And Los Angeles's Koreatown, clocking in at more than two and a half square miles, is without question the mecca of Korean cuisine in all of America. The food served in this vibrant neighborhood, full of tucked-away strip-mall joints and neon lights and late nights spent at karaoke or catching a show at the historic Wiltern theater, is so stellar that even food obsessives visiting from Seoul marvel at its sheer quality and quantity. One could truly spend years trying to eat through all of the restaurants there. Forget about the boundaries between neighborhoods, and just dive in.

1. Badmaash

108 West 2nd Street,
Downtown

This colorful Downtown gastropub serves modern takes on Indian classics in a Bollywood-meets-pop-art space. Founded by chef Pawan Mahendro and sons Nakul and Arjun, Badmaash means "badass," and the menu reflects both the brothers' Indian heritage and childhood in Toronto with dishes like chicken tikka poutine (shown opposite).

2. Bar Amá

118 4th Street,
Downtown

Leave it to San Antonio native and lauded local chef Josef Centeno to introduce LA to Tex-Mex cuisine, which he did when this Downtown stalwart opened in 2012. Known for its Super Nacho Hour and refined snacks (think: vegan queso, puffy fried tacos dorados, turkey albondigas), the allure of this lively minimalist spot endures more than a decade on.

3. Bavel

500 Mateo Street,
Arts District

Bavel, one of the sister restaurants of Ori Menashe and Genevieve Gergis's Bestia, is a love letter to the flavors of the Levant. The gorgeous Arts District space, marked by neutral tones and splashes of greenery, is packed to the rafters nightly with diners happily sharing large platters of lamb neck shawarma and signature dishes like duck 'nduja hummus served with the fluffiest pita bread around.

4. Bestia

2121 East 7th Place,
Arts District

Even though it's been years since Bestia first opened its doors, and essentially single-handedly brought new life to the Arts District, a reservation is still difficult to come by. Clamoring crowds in the sweeping industrial-chic dining room can't get enough of Ori Menashe's rustic Italian pastas and wood-fired meats, as well as Genevieve Gergis's impressive desserts. It's one of LA's most difficult tables to get—and for good reason.

5. Camphor

923 East 3rd Street,
Arts District

Chefs Max Boonthanakit and Lijo George met while working for legendary chef Alain Ducasse and have brought their own of-the-moment take on French-inflected food to the Arts District. The menu at this stunningly elegant (but not stuffy) restaurant zigs from dishes like lobster with coral bisque to a duck-and-beef bar burger on a duck-fat brioche bun.

6. Damian

2132 East 7th Place,
Arts District

Enrique Olvera, widely considered one of Mexico's best chefs, continues to put his distinctive stamp on modern, regional Mexican cuisine at this austere Arts District restaurant anchored by an expansive outdoor patio. That translates to lobster al pastor with pineapple butter, uni tostadas, and carne asada with marrow-roasted leeks. Don't sleep on the cocktails or desserts (and another secret: Olvera's brunch menu is one of the most exciting in town).

7. Danny Boy's Famous Original Pizza

330 South Hope Street,
Downtown

New York City chef Daniel Holzman may have found fame on social media, but the Meatball Shop cofounder is steadily manning the shop at his namesake modern pizzeria in Downtown's Bunker Hill. It's worth the trek to the ground floor of a big office building for some of LA's best New York–style slices.

8. Grand Central Market

317 South Broadway,
Downtown

LA's original food hall is a thriving culinary center in the heart of Downtown, and acts as both a testing ground for up-and-coming chefs and a holdout for long-time vendors. Make sure to check out Sarita's Pupuseria, a classic vendor selling cheese-filled pupusas, Fat + Flour for cookies and pies, and Shiku for affordable Korean home cooking. If you're looking for take-home items, Valeria's Groceries has an impressive selection of Mexican pantry staples including dried chiles, spices, and fresh moles.

9. Han Bat Seol Lung Tang

4163 West 5th Street, Koreatown

This no-frills Koreatown spot specializes in one thing: seolleongtang, or ox bone soup (shown below). The cloudy bone marrow broth here is legendary, as are the tender slabs of brisket and various organ meats floating in it. Build the meal with seasonings, kimchi, and rice, along with a dash of salt and sprinkling of green onions.

10. Kato Restaurant

777 South Alameda Street, Downtown

Chef Jon Yao's Michelin-starred Kato Restaurant is a destination (and one of the toughest reservations in town to score) for its elegant, Taiwanese-influenced tasting menus. A price tag upward of $200 doesn't deter serious diners from splurging on dishes like A5 strip loin, grilled and served with potatoes, black garlic, and braised tendon, served in a beautiful, understated dining room at Row DTLA (page 75).

11. Kobawoo House

698 South Vermont Avenue, Koreatown

Though lunchtime crowds fill this classic, dimly lit dining room housed in a Koreatown strip mall for the bossam, a Korean specialty featuring pork and accouterments, it's worth trying other traditional dishes as well: The hulking seafood pajeon (scallion pancake) is a classic, as is the kimchi stew in a stone pot.

12. Lasita

727 North Broadway, Chinatown

Here's everything you need to know about this lively Filipino restaurant tucked inside the Chinatown shopping center Far East Plaza: It serves natural wine and rotisserie chicken marinated in lemongrass, garlic, spring onion, and ginger in a space that's painted with orange-pink hues inspired by Philippines sunsets. Come for the chicken and stay for the pork belly lechon (crispy-skinned pork belly cooked on the rotisserie) and grilled prawns, and sizzling mushroom sisig laced with red onion and Thai bird chiles.

13. Manuela

907 East 3rd Street, Arts District

Kris Tominaga is behind the stoves at Manuela, the gorgeous indoor-outdoor restaurant inside the Arts District's Hauser & Wirth gallery, which also houses a lovely boutique (page 73). Expect Southern classics with coastal California influences on the menu. The chef's famed biscuits are a must for the table, as are the grilled oysters. Also worth noting: The garden at Manuela has a different menu and a set of cocktails that works great during warm weather.

14. Mapo Dak Galbi

1008 South St. Andrews Place, Koreatown

There's basically one reason to visit this Koreatown classic: large cast-iron pans of spicy dakgalbi placed in the center of a table for everyone to share. The dish develops through the course of the meal, with tender pieces of chicken

thigh, rice cakes, cabbage, and a sweet-spicy sauce that reduces over time. And at the end of the meal, servers take the last portion of each serving and make an amazing seaweed-and-perilla-infused fried rice.

15. MDK Noodles (Myung Dong Kyoja)
3630 Wilshire Boulevard, Koreatown

Formerly known as Myung Dong Kyoja, the easier-to-pronounce MDK has the same carb-laden menu of knife-cut noodles, pork dumplings, and chewy spicy cold noodles called jjolmyeon. All are worth a visit to this casual spot on Wilshire.

16. Mexicali Taco & Co.
702 North Figueroa Street, Downtown

This former street stand turned restaurant by owner Esdras Ochoa puts out incredible tortillas, carne asada, vampiros (a cheese-topped tortilla crisped on the grill, then layered with other toppings), and more done in the Mexicali style of northern Baja. No hype, just delicious food.

17. My Dung Sandwich Shop
314 Ord Street, Chinatown

Amid all the changes in Chinatown over the past decade, there is still My Dung, a timeless, tucked-away banh mi shop. The walk-up restaurant trades in simple and delicious Vietnamese sandwiches, available daily from early in the morning to evening. There may be no better value in all of Chinatown, still.

18. Nick's Cafe
1300 North Spring Street, Chinatown

A staple breakfast destination, not just for Chinatown but for all of Los Angeles, Nick's Cafe is lovingly nicknamed the Ham House on signage out front, dates to 1948, and continues to spin out plates of biscuits, omelets, waffles, apple pie à la mode, and, yes, ham and eggs.

19. Otium
222 South Hope Street, Downtown

Chef Timothy Hollingsworth serves a wide menu of modern American dishes, such as wood-roasted eggplant-and-heirloom tomato tart and a whole grilled branzino and dry-aged duck breast. It's hard to think of a classier place for a date night than this Downtown stunner located steps away from the Broad modern art museum and Walt Disney Concert Hall.

20. Parks BBQ
955 South Vermont Avenue G, Koreatown

This is the premier Korean barbecue restaurant in Koreatown, and Parks delivers with prime-grade meats served at the table, along with a slew of other traditional Korean dishes in a clean, smoke-free environment. The quality of the meat and banchan is simply unsurpassed, rivaling some of the best in Seoul itself. The front parking lot has been converted into an outdoor Korean barbecue setup for additional seating.

21. Philippe The Original
1001 North Alameda Street, Chinatown

There's a reason Philippe uses "the OG" in its social media handles: The iconic restaurant is among LA's oldest, and still draws in tons of adoring fans. People queue up (especially before Dodger games) on the sawdust-covered floors for that famous French dip, which the restaurant claims to have invented (page 100), plus cheap beers and other goodies offered from early morning until night. Grab a jar of the restaurant's signature hot mustard, legendary for its tear-inducing prowess, along with some jarred pickled chile peppers, to go.

22. Pho 87
1019 North Broadway, Chinatown
Pho 87's unfussy Chinatown spot is truly one of the neighborhood's best, and one of the best in the city for slurping noodle-and-herb-filled bowls of pho. Try the #20 with charbroiled pork—but all of their pho features a gorgeous broth.

23. Pizzeria Bianco
1320 East 7th Street, Downtown
Pizza maestro Chris Bianco's industrial-chic spot at Row DTLA opened in 2022, and pizza lovers from near and far have been clamoring for a taste of his lauded pies since. Bianco serves the greatest hits from his original Phoenix location, including small plates like spiedini and antipasti platters, as well as slightly crisp thin-crust pies ranging from Bianco's signature Rosa

pistachio-topped pizza to the Wiseguy, made with wood-roasted onions, smoked mozzarella, and fennel sausage.

24. The Prince
3198½ West 7th Street, Koreatown
Slide into a curved red booth at this Koreatown bar decked out in mid-century furniture that's so slick, the place has been featured in a number of Hollywood productions. Then order up a bevy of bar snacks, including a shatteringly crisp whole Korean fried chicken, kimchi fried rice, and green-onion-studded seafood pancakes. Wash it down with a beer and feel transported to another time.

25. RiceBox
541 South Spring Street, Downtown
This Cantonese barbecue specialist is tucked inside the Spring Arcade at the base of several larger Downtown buildings. What sets RiceBox apart in the preparation of its char siu, bao, and more is its dedication to using only ethically sourced and hormone-free meat.

26. Seong Buk Dong
3303 West 6th Street, Koreatown
This Koreatown restaurant might be on the small side, but it serves up well-crafted traditional dishes with huge flavor. The braised short ribs are a crowd-pleaser, as is the stone pot bibimbap. The spicy braised mackerel is the showstopper, with layers of rich flavor that go perfectly when spooned over multigrain rice.

27. Soban
4001 West Olympic Boulevard, Koreatown

Seafood staple Soban can do no wrong, starting with an amazing array of banchan to begin each meal (shown opposite). The menu features terrific raw crab dressed one of two ways, either in a garlicky soy sauce or thick spicy red pepper sauce. Also try the pan-fried fish and spicy braised black cod or opt for the spicy beef short ribs.

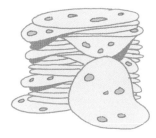

28. Sonoratown
208 East 8th Street, Downtown

This busy Downtown shop decked out in light blue and orange, which also has a Mid-City location, is easily one of the top taco spots in town, serving grilled meats atop perfect tortillas made from Sonoran flour (shown above). Order the shredded beef chivichanga (a dead-simple small burrito filled with meat stewed with tomatoes) and wonder why something so delicious isn't available to every neighborhood in town.

29. Sun Nong Dan
3470 West 6th Street, Koreatown

Koreatown's all-night destination for galbi jjim (braised short ribs) serves it with tender chunks of meat, chewy rice cakes, and tons of spice. While the soups are more than respectable, crowds wait in line outside its strip-mall location for the meat festival served in a stone bowl. Top the galbi jjim with cheese to take it to the next level. There's a big location along Western Avenue as well—in the former Sizzler building.

30. Yang Chow
819 North Broadway, Chinatown

Since 1977, the Yang family has maintained a one-hundred-item menu in the heart of Chinatown. It can be overwhelming, but Yang Chow's staff is helpful in maneuvering diners at tables covered with white tablecloths to the right dishes, including the classic sticky-sweet slippery shrimp (page 101).

QR CODES
for our online guides to these neighborhoods:

ARTS DISTRICT

CHINATOWN

DOWNTOWN

KOREATOWN

DOWNTOWN & KOREATOWN
SHOPPING

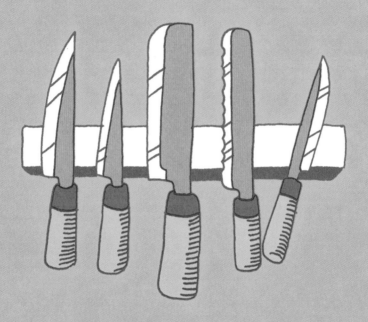

The metropolitan center of Los Angeles spans a fantastic mix of neighborhoods chock-full of culinary shopping gems. The Metro or a rental car makes it possible to see most of the area, which is too vast to explore by foot and includes Little Tokyo, Chinatown, the Arts District, Koreatown, and much more, in a single day. In between scoping out the requisite tourist sites, pencil in a few hours to peek in and peruse these delightful destinations for uniquely LA souvenirs.

1. Anzen Hardware
309 1st Street,
Little Tokyo

From bonsai shears to heritage seeds and chefs' knives, Anzen Hardware is a destination for all things gardening and cooking. With its narrow aisles and tasteful clutter, Anzen has been serving Little Tokyo's Japanese community and beyond since 1946. Aside from the terrific selection of imported Japanese cooking and gardening supplies, the store stocks traditional hardware staples like hammers, nails, screws, keys, and the like.

2. Artbook @ Hauser & Wirth
917 East 3rd Street,
Arts District

Housed in a former flour mill, the Hauser & Wirth gallery hosts an ever-changing lineup of contemporary art exhibitions that are free of charge. Every visit should include a stop at Artbook, the gallery-adjacent shop filled with a great selection of contemporary and twentieth-century art books as well as homewares like blankets, tea towels, dinner plates (some inspired by past and present artworks), and cookbooks penned by Los Angeles–based chefs.

3. Chado Tea Room
369 1st Street,
Little Tokyo

Tea aficionados are sure to be impressed by Chado Tea Room's extensive selection, which includes more than three hundred varieties of loose-leaf brews. If time allows, grab a seat on the outdoor patio of the café/shop tucked inside the Japanese American National Museum for afternoon tea service. For those short on time, purchasing teas to-go is a good option, too. The menu is divided into categories like herbal, jasmine, and matcha, with accompanying succinct descriptions that make navigating the vast tea selection a breeze.

4. Fugetsu-Do
315 1st Street,
Little Tokyo

Established in 1903, Fugetsu-Do is a family-owned and -operated confectionery in Little Tokyo specializing in scratch-made Japanese mochi (a chewy bite-sized dessert made of sweet glutinous rice flour or mochigome) and manju (a small, rounded confection made of wheat, rice flour, and sugar that's stuffed with bean paste, then steamed). The line of sweets includes traditional flavors, like habutai (azuki bean paste) and kiku (chrysanthemum), along with more contemporary takes filled with peanut butter and chocolate ganache. The shop makes a few seasonal items throughout the year, including kuzu manju in July and sakura mochi in early spring.

5. Greenbar Distillery
2459 East 8th Street,
Downtown

Founded by wife-and-husband duo Melkon Khosrovian and Litty Mathew, LA's original distillery boasts the world's largest collection of organic spirits that are all made in Greenbar's Downtown facility. Tours are available periodically and include six sample tastes of the label's offerings. To-go bottles of single malt whiskey and spiced rum are all but guaranteed.

6. Koreatown Galleria
3250 West Olympic Boulevard,
Koreatown

There are plenty of supermarkets in and around Koreatown, but one of the most expansive and impressive sits on the ground floor of the Koreatown Galleria. In addition to shelves chock-full of Korean ingredients and stunningly fresh seafood and produce, the store sells over two dozen house-made banchan sold by weight and packaged to go. Try the pickled perilla leaves or seasoned baby crabs. Also available for takeout are prepared foods like kimchi fried rice and seafood pancakes.

7. LAX-C

1100 North Main Street,
Chinatown

Imagine a giant warehouse on the edge of Chinatown filled with imported ingredients straight from Thailand, and you get LAX-C, or Thai Costco, as regulars call it. Locals in search of curry paste, Jasmine rice, or fresh vegetables sold in bulk come here for its reasonable prices and unparalleled selection. Best of all are the prepared-food stalls both inside and outside the market where vendors sell snacks like grilled meat on a stick, desserts like coconut cream cakes, and other Thai hits for the taking.

8. The Library Store

630 West 5th Street,
Downtown

There are plenty of reasons to swing by the Los Angeles Central Library, from the fabulous architecture (the second-floor Deco-meets-arabesque dome is especially fetching) to the California history mural by Dean Cornwell and the well-curated gift shop. Lining the shelves at the Library Store are Southland-centric mugs, totes, tees, books, and more. Pick up a copy of Josh Kun's *To Live and Dine in L.A.*, which features more than two hundred vintage menus from the library's extensive collection.

9. Now Serving

727 North Broadway,
Chinatown

This jewel-box-sized store hidden away on the ground floor of Far East Plaza in Chinatown is a favorite among local chefs and food lovers for its extensive collection of cookbooks and food magazines. The shop's line of jarred condiments, spices, and sauces formulated by LA chefs make for great gifts or edible souvenirs. Check the shop's calendar, because it often hosts in-person and virtual events with notable culinarians.

10. Olvera Street

845 North Alameda Street,
Downtown

Stroll Olvera Street to get a romanticized sense of what life was like in Los Angeles's earliest days. The tree-lined stretch was created in 1930 as a Mexican marketplace, complete with traditional architecture and a Mexican-style plaza. Today, the painted stalls are occupied by restaurants, cafés, and gift shops selling handcrafted wares (pottery, Mexican folk art, leather goods) and touristy souvenirs. Fuel up on taquitos from Cielito Lindo (page 101) and churros from Mr. Churro while walking the pedestrian-friendly area.

11. Open Market

3339 Wilshire Boulevard,
Koreatown

This neighborhood market and café feels like a love letter to Los Angeles. While the café serves locally roasted coffee and a succinct menu of sandwiches named after LA streets (the Olympic comes with lemongrass chicken, fresh herbs, and fried chicken skin on a baguette), the corner store selection includes hot sauces, chips, and other snacks sourced from mostly local makers.

12. Phoenix Bakery

969 North Broadway,
Chinatown

Stop by this legendary Chinatown bakery for a slice of its famous almond-crusted strawberry layer cake. But don't leave without a box of the shop's equally fantastic almond cookies, which are delicate, crumbly, and just sweet enough, or a few house-made mooncakes, which are available only from late

BEYOND RESTAURANTS

Coffee Shops:
Alchemist Coffee
    Project
Document Coffee Bar
Endorffeine
Verve Coffee Roasters

Bars:
Cafe Brass Monkey
Everson Royce Bar
HMS Bounty
Melody Lounge
The Varnish

Bakeries:
Baker's Bench
Fat + Flour
Pitchoun!
Tous les Jours

Ice Cream:
Bumsam Organic Milk
    Bar
Uli's Gelato

August to early September in honor of the Mid-Autumn Festival.

13. Row DTLA
777 South Alameda Street,
Downtown

Weekdays at Row DTLA are quiet, but the place lights up on Sunday, when the former American Apparel factory grounds play host to weekly food festival Smorgasburg. No matter when you can drop by, the concentration of well-curated shops with an eye toward local artisans makes it worth a visit. A stop into Flask & Field is a must for those who love wine, spirits, art, and design, and where bottles of made-in-LA Future Gin make for a tremendous gift or souvenir. Nearby Still Life Ceramics sells everyday kitchen and homewares crafted by local artists.

14. Utsuwa-No-Yakata
333 Alameda Street,
Little Tokyo

Step inside Little Tokyo's "house of pottery" for an impressive selection of Japanese ceramics. Products range from standard plates, glasses, and bowls to dedicated wares intended for tea and sake service and even bento boxes. Founded in 1981, Utsuwa-No-Yakata sources its line of both traditional and contemporary goods directly from Japan and proudly carries bespoke products that are handmade in small kilns.

A PERFECT TWENTY-FOUR HOURS (AND THEN SOME) IN LA

By Matthew Kang

Los Angeles is a huge metropolitan area, and navigating the tangle of busy streets and freeways is daunting even for a local, but the journey is part of the fun—and the only way to access some of the most diverse and well-prepared food on the planet. You could, of course, spend a lifetime eating in Los Angeles and never get bored, but if you have only one day, and can maybe stretch it to two, this is how to optimize your time.

We're starting in Hollywood, making our way to Silver Lake, then hitting Chinatown, Downtown, and Koreatown before calling it a night.

Just a few notes about getting around LA: First, it's really best to have a car, but a combination of walking, public transit, ridesharing, and even cycling can make most of these destinations accessible. So don't feel discouraged. Distances between each location aren't more than a few miles.

8:00 A.M.

Los Angeles is a city that loves breakfast. Maybe it's because there are so many aspiring actors, freelancers, and young folks who don't need to rush into offices, or that the often-hazy morning sun beckons the hungover and the hungry to seek out pancakes and eggs, but greasy spoons and diners are consistently packed. **Clark Street Diner** (page 89) is a revitalized classic of a Hollywood diner that lived for decades as 101 Coffee Shop. The scene inside feels entirely cinematic, with its long sight lines, midcentury feel, sassy service, and reliable menu of breakfast sandwiches, griddled meats, and crisp waffles. Imagine the opening scenes of *Pulp Fiction* or *Reservoir Dogs*, both of which have pivotal scenes in LA diners. Clark Street Diner is the perfect place to relive those scenes, with strong coffee, good banter, and a side of creamer.

Clark Street Diner
6145 Franklin Avenue, Hollywood

9:00 A.M.

Most people won't need to eat again after a morning at Clark Street Diner, but **Roscoe's House of Chicken N Waffles** (page 130) is such a Hollywood soul-food institution that it demands to be the second meal of the morning. Make the half-mile trek down Gower to arrive at Roscoe's, where you can expect heaping platters of crisp golden-brown fried chicken draped over supple, thinner-than-expected Southern-style waffles. Douse with maple syrup for the complete experience.

Roscoe's House of Chicken N Waffles
1514 N Gower Street, Hollywood

10:30 A.M.

Savor the heart of Hollywood and the iconic Walk of Fame to see how many celebrities of yore you can remember. The somewhat grungy area is littered with tattoo parlors, trinket shops, and pizza slice spots, but it's worth exploring midmorning. Check out the closest thing

LA has to Times Square in front of the Chinese Theater, then point your GPS to Thai Town, located just east of Hollywood and home to the country's first concentration of Thai American restaurants and businesses. Tucked into the prime strip mall and surrounded by numerous colorful places to eat is the tiny but mighty **Bhan Kanom Thai** (page 40), a dessert specialist that serves fragrant discs of chewy purple coconut taro cakes called pang chi that are griddled hot and fresh. Bhan Kanom Thai has various dried snacks, milk teas, and other Thai sweets that are difficult to find elsewhere, all at fairly budget prices. The warm melt-in-your-mouth kanom krok, or custardy coconut rice flour cakes, are another must-order when they're fresh. The dessert store also acts as a place to send remittances to Thailand or exchange baht to US dollars. How many other dessert shops offer financial services to go along with tasty sweets? Afterward, wander outside and take in the weathered signage and wafts of jasmine in Thai Town to experience one of LA's finest Asian enclaves.

Bhan Kanom Thai
5271 Hollywood Boulevard, East Hollywood

11:30 A.M.

At this point, it's difficult to fathom anyone having much of an appetite, but there's nothing more quintessentially LA than standing in line for an au courant food item that begs to be posted on Instagram. While Virgil Village's first big star, **Sqirl**, contended with some issues of recipe credit and food safety issues in the past, most of the neighborhood has quietly crept back for jam-laden ricotta toast. But the lines have since moved over to **Courage Bagels**. There, Ari Skye makes naturally fermented Montreal-style bagels featuring marvelous, airy crumbs with crispier outsides than the more common New York City variety. Most folks order the toasted bagels smeared with cream cheese, topped with lox and a tuft of dill. You can also top the bagels with bright red salmon roe pearls or slices of supremely ripe heirloom tomatoes with paper-thin coins of crisp cucumber. Grab a stool, gawk at the well-dressed crowd waiting in line, and soak in the breezy vibes feeling like a true Angeleno.

Sqirl
720 North Virgil Avenue, Virgil Village/ Silver Lake

Courage Bagels
777 North Virgil Avenue, Virgil Village/ Silver Lake

12:00 P.M.

Next, get a sense of the spirit of LA's stylish eastern food scene at **Pine & Crane** (page 38). Founded by astute first-time restaurateur Vivian Ku, the restaurant serves everyday Taiwanese fare in a relaxed café setting and is named after Ku's grandfather's former noodle factory in Taiwan. Ku sources greens—like pea sprouts, sauteed simply with oil and garlic—from her family farm in Central California. The menu features plenty of crowd-pleasing options, from nutty dan dan noodles or juicy shrimp wontons to the syrupy, savory, and slightly sweet three-cup chicken served with a pile of steamed white rice. Don't miss an order of boba tea with a scoop of egg pudding, or maybe a dessert of freshly made chewy hakka mochi topped with crushed black sesame seeds and peanuts.

Pine & Crane
1521 Griffith Park Boulevard, Silver Lake

1:30 P.M.

While specialty coffee seems ubiquitous in LA, the dining scene was a much different place in 2007 when Intelligentsia landed at this airy space in Silver Lake's Sunset Junction. Before Intelligentsia opened, the city hadn't seen prototypical early-aughts baristas wearing suspenders and beanies. Serving some of the country's best coffee in an indoor-outdoor café, Intelligentsia was a place where writers, actors, producers, and anyone aspiring to do something in this city would gather. And after a decade and a half, **Intelligentsia Coffee's Silver Lake Coffeebar** still feels like that timeless neighborhood coffee spot that helped fuel a thousand dreams. Order a latte and sit on the back counter for people-watching perfection. After the caffeine break, take a stroll in any direction in Sunset Junction— LA's hipster ground zero—and find everything from overpriced boutiques to comic book shops to fetish leather stores. If you're feeling ambitious, walk farther east down Sunset to see the remnants of Elliott Smith's famous *Figure 8* mural.

Intelligentsia Coffee's Silver Lake Coffeebar
3922 Sunset Boulevard, Silver Lake

2:00 P.M.

If the stroll around Sunset Junction wasn't enough, there are three public parks in the area to help digest and burn some calories. **Echo Park Lake** is a picturesque place with clear views of Downtown. **Vista Hermosa** has been the site of numerous films and TV shows because of its unfettered views of the city. **Elysian Park** is a bit farther out, but **Buena Vista View Point** is a terrific place to catch sweeping views of the Downtown and LA river areas. One thing many people forget is that unlike other large American cities, Los Angeles is surrounded by hills and mountains, making it perfect for urban hiking. (Speaking of which: Hit the trails at **Runyon Canyon** or **Griffith Park** for people-watching as good as the scenery.)

2:30 P.M.

From any of the prior three parks, LA's Chinatown is just a short drive, transit ride, or walk away. While this Chinatown is quite old, with historic buildings that go back decades, the city's original Chinatown was actually where Union Station stands now. That was demolished to give way to the current neighborhood dotted with sidewalk stores, ornate Chinese buildings, and a dense cluster of Cantonese and Vietnamese restaurants. Be sure to stop by the tiny **My Dung Sandwich Shop** (page 69) for a super-affordable Vietnamese sandwich. The bánh mì dac biet blends pickled vegetables with cold cuts. As in any Chinatown in the US, sundry street shops sell trinkets, mementos, and even produce, making it a good place to pick up affordable souvenirs.

And for those wondering, the real hub of Chinese American culture in Los Angeles moved years ago to the eastern suburbs of the San Gabriel Valley, itself a destination for great Asian food (see pages 55–57).

My Dung Sandwich Shop
314 Ord Street, Chinatown

4:30 P.M.

Just a few miles south of Chinatown and a short train ride away, **Grand Central Market** (page 67) stands as a testament to Downtown's long history. Going back more than one hundred years, this food hall and grocery has changed with the times, but you'll still find many old-school vendors selling candies and fresh produce along with chef-run stalls doing everything from egg sandwiches and vegan ramen to fresh pasta plates and Filipino rice bowls. It's a terrific place to meander, soak in the smells and sights of LA's original food hall, and maybe taste a few bites. The cookies and pies at **Fat + Flour** from chef Nicole Rucker are especially fantastic, along with the modern Korean doshirak (bento boxes) from chef Kwang Uh of **Shiku**. **Sarita's**, one of the classic vendors, makes amazing cheesy pupusas stuffed with loroco, a Salvadoran herb.

Grand Central Market
317 South Broadway, Downtown

6:00 P.M.

It's difficult to fathom that it's this late in the day and you haven't yet had a taco, Los Angeles's most iconic food. Remember that LA was once part of the Spanish colony of Mexico, and part of the country of Mexico until the Mexican-American War. As a result, Mexican cuisine and culture are imbued in every part of the city. **Sonoratown** (page 71), from founders Teodoro Diaz-Rodriguez Jr. and Jennifer Feltham, is named after the former neighborhood of Mexicans from Sonora that lived in what is now Chinatown. This versatile taco restaurant makes some of the finest flour tortillas anywhere, which work fantastically as vehicles for chorizo or grilled steak, though everyone is keen on ordering at least one chivichanga here. The miniature burrito made with the thin flour tortilla comes stuffed with chicken or beef, smoky Anaheim chile, and a guisado, or stew, of jack cheese, cheddar, and blistered tomato.

Sonoratown
5610 San Vicente Boulevard, Downtown

7:00 P.M.

You've probably had enough food for a while, so it's time to sit back and enjoy a great view at the Freehand hotel, which has a relaxed rooftop branch of Miami's famous **Broken Shaker** bar with nearly unfettered views of Downtown. The Exchange Building that houses the hotel and Broken Shaker was built in 1924 and features one of the tallest neon signs in Downtown along the street corner. The rooftop kind of feels like a kooky neighbor's backyard, with tropical-ish foliage, mismatched furniture, and a pool that no one seems to swim in, giving the impression of a more approachable, less snooty urban lounge experience. And the drinks are creative, crushable, and ever-changing, with concoctions like a gin, framboise, and elderflower tonic sipper called the LA Breeze and a mezcal, suze, kiwi, and sorrel spritzer called the Thirst Trap.

Broken Shaker
416 West 8th Street, Downtown

8:30 P.M.

It's hard to think of a neighborhood in the United States that has undergone such a radical change in recent years as Downtown's Arts District. That said, before **Bestia** (page 67) opened, the area, known for its industrial warehouses and manufacturing facilities and named for an influx of artists in the 1970s who took advantage of the area's affordable rents, was basically forgotten by most visitors and Angelenos alike.

But Bestia, which indeed occupies a former industrial building, is one of the most important and talked-about restaurants to open in LA in the past fifteen years. That's due to the sheer energy and incredible brio that pours out of this space from the roaring crowd of eager diners, many of whom have waited weeks to score a reservation or arrived right at five P.M. to beg for a walk-in seat. Bestia could be labeled a California Italian restaurant, but chef Ori Menashe and wife Genevieve Gergis (who handles the desserts) have created an institution that defies simple labels. Menashe makes his own dry salumi on the premises, a true rarity, and the board of thinly sliced pork products is a masterpiece of aged meats. All the dishes amplify umami and deliciousness to the nth degree, from the 'nduja-tinted mussels and dry-aged beef crostini to black truffle cavatelli with pork sausage. To finish, try Gergis's salty chocolate budino tart or spiced chestnut zeppole with coffee ice cream.

9:45 P.M.

It's time to head over to Koreatown, one of the first-ever enclaves dedicated to Korean culture and cuisine in the United States. Though Koreans have been in Los Angeles since the early 1900s, Koreatown wasn't established until immigration waves in the 1960s brought numerous Korean immigrants to Wilshire Center, a business district that boasted some of the swankiest Hollywood destinations, including the Ambassador Hotel and its Cocoanut Grove and the famed Brown Derby restaurant. Since the 1960s, Korean American businesses and eating establishments have dominated the area, which comprises one of the most diverse and densely populated neighborhoods in Los Angeles. Today, the population of nearly three hundred thousand includes Koreans, Mexicans, Guatemalans, Salvadorans, Oaxacans, and Bangladeshi, as well as plenty of transplants who appreciate the thriving scene.

Sul & Beans, one of South Korea's most popular dessert spots, offers freshly cooked red beans served atop a perfect mound of shaved ice called patbingsoo. Koreans love to enjoy red bean shaved ice with toppings, so pick a combination that works for your mood, from mango to strawberry to matcha.

Sul & Beans
621 South Western Avenue, Koreatown

11:00 P.M.

No visit to Los Angeles is complete without a raucous night at **Dan Sung Sa**, one of the city's most storied Korean drinking establishments. Walk into the dimly lit space to find a center kitchen spitting out steaming-hot plates of bean sprout soup, bossam, boiled silkworm larvae, and grilled meat skewers. Dan Sung Sa is the best place to pile in, down ice-cold soju shots, and sip on refreshing Korean beer. The walls and wooden barriers feature drunken love notes, salutations, and scratched-on ephemera, adding to the charm of this bar. As the night goes on, enjoy the textbook Korean combination of faultless drinking food and easy-drinking booze.

Dan Sung Sa
3317 West 6th Street, Koreatown

12:30 A.M.

For one last tipple, venture back to Downtown, where you'll walk into **Cole's**, one of the two restaurants that claim to have invented the French dip sandwich. Look for the barely marked door in the back to open a portal into Downtown LA's timeless speakeasy **The Varnish**. This was the place where legendary New York City bartender Sasha Petraske left his mark, opening the place with bar veteran Eric Alperin in 2009. Since then, cocktail culture has blossomed in Los Angeles, but the Varnish was always the place that perfected the basics, cutting its own crystal-clear ice and offering a tight set of daily drinks, from a gin-lemon Business cocktail to a shaken Ramos Gin Fizz. The tiny room featuring minuscule tables feels like

the place where flappers and suited folk would squeeze in maybe a hundred years ago during Prohibition. It certainly helps that the building, a former streetcar train station built in 1905, carries its own history. A favorite of the late critic Jonathan Gold, this intimate, near-hidden room works as a contemplative coda to an epic day of eating and drinking through Los Angeles.

Cole's and the Varnish
118 Eest 6th Street, Downtown

1:30 A.M.

But wait—no LA food tour would be complete without a stop at a taco truck, some of which stay open until two A.M. to supply the city's night owls with sustenance. Bop up to nearby Echo Park to seek out the **Leo's Tacos** truck there (page 105), one of nine the popular purveyor has parked around the city. Stave off a hangover with the al pastor: The spit-roasted pork is served topped with a flurry of chopped onions and cilantro. Hydrate with a jamaica agua fresca and congratulate yourself on a day well spent.

Beverly Grove
Fairfax
Hollywood
Little Ethiopia
Mid-Wilshire
Miracle Mile
West Hollywood

CENTI

4

RALLA

CENTRAL LA

DINING

1. ABSteak
2. Angelini Osteria
3. A.O.C.
4. Canter's
5. Chi Spacca
6. Clark Street Diner
7. Connie and Ted's
8. Dan Tana's
9. Gigi's
10. Irv's Burgers
11. Jon & Vinny's Fairfax
12. Luv2eat Thai Bistro
13. Madre
14. Melanie Wine Bar
15. Merois
16. Mother Wolf
17. Mr. T
18. The Musso & Frank Grill
19. Night + Market
20. Pizzana
21. Providence
22. République
23. Ronan
24. Salt's Cure
25. Slab
26. Sunset Tower
27. Sushi Tama
28. Tail o' the Pup

SHOPPING

1. Academy Museum Store
2. Bottega Louie
3. Buna Ethiopian Restaurant & Market
4. Dacha
5. Go Get Em Tiger
6. Heath Ceramics
7. Hollywood Farmers' Market
8. Jenni Kayne
9. Joan's on Third
10. Lawson-Fenning
11. Nickey Kehoe
12. OK
13. Standing's Butchery
14. TableArt
15. The Original Farmers Market
16. Slammers Cafe at Brain Dead Studios
17. Vromage

CENTRAL LA
DINING

Now we've made it to a large central swath of Los Angeles, a region that, for our purposes, includes all of Hollywood, Beverly Grove, Mid-Wilshire, the Miracle Mile, and Fairfax. In addition to having some of the city's most iconic landmarks—this is, after all, the land of the Walk of Fame and the Hollywood Bowl—Hollywood is full of glitzy celebrity hot spots and old-school restaurants you've undoubtedly seen in the movies, like the Musso & Frank Grill (hello, *Once Upon a Time in Hollywood*). West Hollywood, known for its vibrant LGBTQ+ communities, chic hotels, and lively bar scene, is home to some of the city's most stylish eateries, which deliver on much more than ambience alone.

Meanwhile, Beverly Grove, Mid-Wilshire, and the Miracle Mile, all located near the shopping mecca The Grove, offer a bevy of well-heeled boutiques and dining options. Over on hip Fairfax, you'll see youngsters lined up for the latest release at the area's impossibly cool streetwear boutiques, and you'll find restaurants that range from storied Jewish delis to new-school classics like Cofax and Jon & Vinny's.

And, of course, this being Los Angeles, interwoven among all of that are Armenian bakeries, dim sum, and even healthy Japanese fare. And did we mention that Thai Town, just east of Hollywood, has some of the best Thai food in the entire country?

1. ABSteak

8500 Beverly Boulevard,
Beverly Grove

Akira Back, a Korean-born chef who runs a global empire of upscale Asian restaurants, offers a fully formed modern Korean barbecue restaurant in a sweeping, dramatic space in Beverly Grove. The menu features expertly dry-aged meats, Wagyu cuts, a polished but tight set of banchan, and traditionally Korean sides like mini seafood pancakes and tofu jjigae. Unlike its more casual brethren like Parks (page 69) or Baekjeong (page 51), ABSteak might be the ultimate in luxury Korean barbecue. The ABSteak grand beef short rib galbi is the best overall cut and priced at $65 a serving.

2. Angelini Osteria

7313 Beverly Boulevard,
Beverly Grove

This casually elegant restaurant, with its exposed-brick dining room and high ceilings, is a Beverly Boulevard legend thanks to Italian-born chef Gino Angelini and his incredible pasta-making skills. From the restaurant's signature lemon cream pasta to ones made with sea urchin, this is a true pasta haven. The fried-basil-topped lasagna is notable as well. Save room for simple desserts like affogato and chocolate budino.

3. A.O.C.

8700 West 3rd Street,
West Hollywood

Helmed by the James Beard Award–winning team of Suzanne Goin and Caroline Styne, the iconic, twenty-plus-year-old restaurant located on an upmarket stretch of West Hollywood is known for its French-leaning fare, robust wine list, chic dining room, and gorgeous garden. Dishes like spiced fish tagine and hanger steak with a harissa butter have become the blueprint for countless other restaurants in the city and around the country.

4. Canter's

417 North Fairfax Avenue,
Fairfax

Although you can find better deli food around town, the ambience at this Fairfax mainstay is hard to beat, making it worth a visit in the middle of the night when the city dies down. Night owls have gathered under the restaurant's colorful, weird ceilings for generations, to catch up over corned beef Reubens, matzo ball soup, and the like.

5. Chi Spacca

6610 Melrose Avenue,
Hollywood

Part of the multi-pronged Mozza complex (page 104), this indulgent Italian-style steakhouse is an essential destination for the bistecca fiorentina, a 50-ounce dry-aged prime porterhouse. For those feeling skittish, there's the costata alla fiorentina, a prime dry-aged, bone-in New York steak that registers only 36 ounces. The intimate restaurant is a meat lover's paradise, but save room for the cheese-filled focaccia di recco.

6. Clark Street Diner

6145 Franklin Avenue,
Hollywood

The beloved 101 Coffee Shop, a Hollywood diner made famous for its background role in the film *Swingers*, was taken over by local bakery Clark Street Bread in 2021. Owner Zack Hall made the place even better, with great coffee, fluffy pancakes, plentiful pastry, and patty melts in a buzzy room outfitted with a long counter and classic leather booths.

7. Connie and Ted's

8171 Santa Monica Boulevard,
West Hollywood

Providence (page 92) chef Michael Cimarusti serves classic New England–style dishes, pristine oysters, and a mean blondie sundae for dessert at his slightly more casual restaurant Connie and Ted's, which remains one of the top seafood restaurants in Los Angeles. The patio overlooking bustling Santa Monica Boulevard is an especially good place for people-watching.

8. Dan Tana's
9071 Santa Monica Boulevard, West Hollywood

This long-standing West Hollywood red-sauce joint, complete with red-and-white checkered table-cloths, is as old-school as it gets. Although the restaurant's conspicuous preference to seat regulars and celebrities over nobodies can make snagging a table difficult even with a reservation, the chicken parm and the strong martinis are worth the hassle. Expect large portions, waiters in

jackets, and classic flour-ishes like a Caesar mixed tableside.

9. Gigi's
904 North Sycamore Avenue, Hollywood

This upscale French bistro serves excellent cocktails, oysters, and luxe takes on classics like steak tartare in a sexy dining room with gilded and midcentury accents. There's also a giant, bustling patio that looks out onto a stretch of Sycamore Street that's become a dining and shopping hot spot in recent years.

10. Irv's Burgers
1000 South La Brea Avenue, West Hollywood

After a four-year shut-down, this classic burger favorite reopened at a new location a few blocks away from its West Hollywood

original. The menu offers the beloved no-nonsense Irv's Single (with cheese, lettuce, tomatoes, onions, pickles, ketchup, mayo, and mustard), as well as a pared-down Just For You burger (with cheese, Thousand Island dress-ing, and thick pickles on a seeded proprietary bun). This being a burger stand, there are fries and milk-shakes, too.

11. Jon & Vinny's Fairfax
412 North Fairfax Avenue, Fairfax

After hitting it big with the now-shuttered Animal and their seafood restaurant Son of a Gun, chef duo Jon Shook and Vinny Dotolo took on red sauce with Jon & Vinny's. Now a chain with locations all over the city, the Fairfax original is still a solid go-to for thin-crust pizza (like the dead-simple LA Woman, topped with tomato sauce and burrata) and chicken parm at night and a surprisingly robust breakfast and lunch menu.

12. Luv2eat Thai Bistro
6660 Sunset Boulevard, Hollywood

A casual Thai restaurant located in a run-down strip mall isn't unusual in Thai Town, but this spot stands out for its well-executed Southern Thai cooking. The Phuket-style crab curry, jade noodles, and hat yai fried chicken are popular with regulars. It's constantly busy, and doesn't take reservations, so you may be there awhile.

13. Madre
801 North Fairfax Avenue, West Hollywood
This mini chain of modern Mexican restaurants, with locations in West Hollywood, Palms, and Torrance, is known for excellent Oaxacan fare. The WeHo location also happens to have the largest selection of mezcal in the country, so you're going to want to try the smoky spirit in a flight or a cocktail. Pair your drink with anything featuring one of the house-made moles.

14. Melanie Wine Bar
8310 West 3rd Street, Beverly Grove
A moody wine bar situated on the posh dining and shopping stretch of West Third Street, Melanie is a place for simple French and Italian fare to go along with terrific wines by the glass. Slide into the long banquette or grab a seat at the cozy marble-topped counter to try a chilled red Morgon from Domaine Bulliat or a sparkling Crémant due Jura from Domaine Rolet to go with salt spring mussels or charred Spanish octopus.

15. Merois
8430 Sunset Boulevard West Hollywood
In 2021, Wolfgang Puck returned triumphantly to the LA dining scene, opening a pair of restaurants for the first time in more than a decade. Perched atop the Pendry West Hollywood hotel, the opulent Merois is awash in neutral tones, offering swoon-worthy floor-to-ceiling views of the city below. Puck's menu combines Japanese, Southeast Asian, and French/California influences, kicking off with dim sum like a lobster spring roll with sweet chili sauce, then moves on to bintochan-grilled Spanish octopus and mains like Beijing duck for two.

16. Mother Wolf
1545 Wilcox Avenue, Hollywood
Take a few minutes to observe the opulent dining room at Hollywood's Mother Wolf, handmade pasta impresario Evan Funke's love letter to Rome. There's a lot to take in, with the sweeping ceilings, roomy red leather booths, and elegant chandeliers. The equally upscale menu offers Funke's take on classics like cacio e pepe, wood-fired pizza, and a sixty-day dry-aged rib eye. Be on the lookout for the digestivo drink cart.

17. Mr. T
953 North Sycamore Avenue, Hollywood
A true French import—Mr. T has combined French technique with stylized versions of global street food in Paris's Marais district since 2017—this relative newcomer to the Hollywood Media District combines an industrial-chic space with playful high-concept dishes like BBQ chips served with truffle cream, or a signature mac and cheese with Comté cheese flambé.

18. The Musso & Frank Grill
6667 Hollywood Boulevard, Hollywood
Martinis done right and a menu that's barely changed since opening day have kept this Hollywood restaurant running since 1919. Grab a booth and dig into a menu of continental favorites that reads like yesteryear. Think mushrooms on toast, lobster thermidor, and turkey à la king. And there are plenty of hulking steaks and chops on offer, too.

19. Night + Market
9043 Sunset Boulevard West, West Hollywood
Come to the original Night + Market in West Hollywood for some superb Thai cooking, a cold beer, and a technicolor atmosphere. Chef Kris Yenbamroong's menu includes Thai classics and lesser-known regional specialties. The pork toro

and lunch are constant but well worth the wait. Approaching République for dinner is best with reservations, which will ensure a faster route to dishes like oysters, roast chicken, duck breast, and house-made bread with pan drippings, served in a gorgeous Spanish-style brick building on bustling La Brea that was originally built for Charlie Chaplin.

is a must-order, along with the khao soi and crispy rice salad. Additional locations of Night + Market include Venice (page 149), Silver Lake, and the Virgin Hotels in Las Vegas.

20. Pizzana
460 North Robertson Boulevard, West Hollywood
Naples-born pizzaiolo Daniele Uditi makes what's widely considered some of the best pizza in Los Angeles at the second location of Pizzana, a mostly outdoor sit-down situation on a retail-heavy stretch of Robertson in West Hollywood. He uses organic, stone-ground Italian flour and a forty-eight-hour fermentation process to produce traditional Neapolitan pies. The cacio e pepe and neo margherita (topped with San Marzano tomato, fior di latte cheese, Parmesan, and dehydrated and fresh

basil) are sure bets, while the lunchtime sandwiches are also fantastic.

21. Providence
5955 Melrose Avenue, Hollywood
One of the few examples of true fine dining in Los Angeles, Providence serves one of the most beautiful tasting menus in the city, with a focus on artfully prepared, sparklingly fresh seafood. It's packed almost every single evening, thanks to Michael Cimarusti's exceptional cooking that is matched only by Donato Poto's warm and efficient service in a dining room that's elegant without feeling stuffy.

22. République
624 South La Brea Avenue, Mid-Wilshire
Although it's been around for a decade, République is as popular as ever. The weekend lines for breakfast

23. Ronan
7315 Melrose Avenue, West Hollywood
The husband-and-wife team behind West Hollywood's Ronan have an incredible Italian-inspired restaurant that offers perfectly blistered wood-fired pizza and so much more, from creative salads and starters like a triumphant chicken liver pâté to excellent entrees like a seabass zarandeado served "banchan-style." Don't sleep on the cocktails, all served in vintage glassware.

24. Salt's Cure
1155 North Highland Avenue, Hollywood
Neighborhood staple and brunch favorite Salt's Cure does the simple things really well, with an amazing set of oatmeal pancakes and biscuits and gravy for breakfast, decadent sandwiches at lunch, and a renowned pork chop at dinner. The service is as warm

as the restaurant, done up in light wood, with plenty of sunshine streaming in from large windows looking out onto Highland Avenue.

25. Slab
8136 West 3rd Street, Beverly Grove

Slab serves solid versions of all the barbecue classics in a casual, order-at-the-counter setup in Beverly Grove: Go for the spare ribs, smoked chicken, brisket, brisket burgers (shown above), and sides like mac and cheese. But it's more than just the basics here. Chef Burt Bakman embraces experimentation with an ever-changing slate of spices and sauces, many of which are available bottled to take home.

26. Sunset Tower
8358 Sunset Boulevard, West Hollywood

A whole new generation of aspirational Angelenos are rediscovering Sunset Tower's energetic pull. Part see-and-be-seen destination, part Hollywood schmooze-fest, part laid-back hotel bar and swank restaurant, this hotel restsaurant is the spot to show off on a date or have a celebratory meal. Just don't be surprised if a few well-heeled celebrities are seated nearby (and because of the celeb factor, note that you aren't allowed to take photos, so keep those cell phones tucked away).

27. Sushi Tama
116 North Robertson Boulevard, West Hollywood/Beverly Grove

Sushi Tama opened in August 2020 with a sleek counter and impeccable nigiri using Japanese-sourced fish. Chef Hideyuki Yoshimoto worked for years in Tokyo's Tsukiji fish market before partnering with Shōwa Hospitality at this stylish sushi destination in a chic part of West Hollywood/Beverly Grove.

28. Tail o' the Pup
8512 Santa Monica Boulevard, West Hollywood

What could be more LA than getting a hot dog at a retro-styled stand shaped like an actual hot dog? West Hollywood's iconic Tail o' the Pup, originally built in 1946 but reopened in 2022 at a new location on Santa Monica Boulevard, offers, yes, plenty of hot dogs, but also burgers, fries, soft serve, milkshakes, and beer and wine. (You may have spotted the stand in movies like *Body Double* and *LA Story*, by the way.)

QR CODES
for our online guides to these neighborhoods:

HOLLYWOOD

WEST HOLLYWOOD

CENTRAL LA
SHOPPING

The sheer diversity of food-related shopping options in this part of town is enough to make one's head spin and belly growl. Amid gated movie studios and contemporary museums, find tropical Thai desserts, gorgeous tableware, and even whimsical chocolate bars for the taking. There's much to discover and bring home across these busy boulevards and tree-lined neighborhoods.

1. Academy Museum Store
6067 Wilshire Boulevard
Miracle Mile
The Academy Museum Store, which is a part of the Academy Museum of Motion Pictures, isn't your average museum gift shop. With its 2,600-square-foot (240-square-meter) footprint, the store stocks unique merchandise designed and produced exclusively for the museum, located west of Koreatown in Mid-Wilshire. From items for the office and home to posters, maps, and toys, there's something for every cinephile among the enormous and eclectic array. Be on the lookout for specialty items made by Los Angeles– and California-based artists and designers.

2. Bottega Louie
8936 Santa Monica Boulevard
West Hollywood
Make a pit stop for sweets at this gorgeous patisserie. While the original location in Downtown boasts a grand, almost stately interior, the West Hollywood outlet is breezier, with a casual indoor-outdoor footprint that's perfect for the neighborhood. The house-made French macarons, which come in flavors like strawberry, violet cassis, matcha, lemon, salted caramel, and espresso, make for splendid gifts. Or linger awhile with a flat white and an almost-too-pretty-to-eat eclair or fruit tart.

3. Buna Ethiopian Restaurant & Market
1034 South Fairfax Avenue
Little Ethiopia
Little Ethiopia, which sits west of Koreatown on Fairfax Avenue, is a bustling stretch of Ethiopian-owned restaurants and stores. Buna Ethiopian Restaurant & Market opened in 2011 and stocks imported handicrafts, groceries, and, best of all, Yirgacheffe coffee beans sourced from Southern Ethiopia. The beans are brewed on-site and available for purchase in one-pound bags or in bulk. If time allows, take a respite from the grind with a slice of house-made tiramisu—a culinary remnant from Italy's brief occupation of Ethiopia during World War II—paired with a mug of coffee.

4. Dacha
420 North Robertson Boulevard, West Hollywood

Set in the West Hollywood Design District, Dacha's flagship store is brimming with home accessories, furniture, pillows, and covetable objects. The store's founder and owner, Lauren Gregory, brings together a lovely collection that balances California cool with global influences. In between the vintage and new finds are works from California-based artists and designers, as well as gifts priced at $20 and up, like plants, candles, and artisanal chocolates. Find an additional Dacha location in Manhattan Beach.

5. Go Get Em Tiger
8253 Santa Monica Boulevard, West Hollywood

Kyle Glanville and Charles Babinski are the undisputed kings of third-wave coffee in Los Angeles. In addition to their original stall, G&B Coffee, inside Downtown's Grand Central Market (page 67), Glanville operates almost a dozen Go Get Em Tiger shops throughout the Southland. It's easy to caffeinate well here, but don't miss the selection of well-designed merch (T-shirts, hats, totes, mugs), along with the twelve-ounce bags of coffee beans available for home brewing.

6. Heath Ceramics
7525 Beverly Boulevard, Mid-Wilshire

The Northern California–based ceramicist beloved by chefs and home cooks has a retail store in Mid-Wilshire. In addition to carrying its own line of dinnerware, vases, and the like, the shop also stocks beautifully designed home goods from LA artists, such as the hand-dyed textiles (tablecloths, table runners, napkins) from Cathy Callahan and hand-blown glass vessels from Cedric Mitchell. Scope out the in-house gallery, Clay Studio, for inspiring exhibits featuring various artists, makers, and thinkers.

7. Hollywood Farmers' Market
1600 Ivar Avenue, Hollywood

Come Sundays in Hollywood, more than 150 of Southern California's finest farmers, producers, and food artisans set up shop at the intersection of Selma and Ivar for one of the most vibrant outdoor marketplaces around. Beginning at eight A.M. and running until one P.M., the weekly gathering boasts pristine produce, along with wonderful food products made by local artisans, like Bearclaw Kitchen's granola and Bezian Bakery's wild yeast breads. The market's family-friendly atmosphere attracts a great crowd from start to finish.

8. Jenni Kayne
614 North Almont Drive, West Hollywood

Trust Los Angeles fashion designer and lifestyle guru Jenni Kayne when it comes to capturing a genuine West Coast feel at home. From casual decor to kitchen and dining essentials, her West Hollywood showroom is all about that laid-back yet luxe LA vibe. Even simple kitchen staples like cutting boards, canisters, and coasters exude a kind of effortless cool that brings a little bit of Los Angeles into every home.

9. Joan's on Third

8350 West 3rd Street,
Beverly Grove

This Beverly Grove staple's been around since 1998 and remains the go-to market-place for gourmet goodies, an easy coffee meetup, or daytime noshing. The three-thousand-square-foot emporium includes a well-stocked bakery, soft-serve, olive bar, and cheese counter, but it's Joan's selection of well-curated food products that makes it a wonderland for shopping. Find locally sourced, as well as internationally imported food products, that make for excellent gifts. On the way out, grab a magic bar with caramel, pecans, and chocolate chips to go. Also check out their additional location in Studio City.

10. Nickey Kehoe

7266 Beverly Boulevard,
Mid-Wilshire

To bring some of that California-cool design aesthetic back home, head to Mid-Wilshire, where Todd Nickey and Amy Kehoe stock a retail shop filled with highly covetable wares. The LA-based design duo's showroom includes big-ticket items like couches and coffee tables, as well as more approachable home and kitchen accessories that can easily fit into a carry-on, like tea towels, dinnerware, and ceramics.

11. Lawson-Fenning

6824 Melrose Avenue,
Hollywood

The two-story flagship showroom for Los Angeles–based designers Glenn Lawson and Grant Fenning includes locally made furniture, lighting, and accessories designed by the duo. Lawson-Fenning supplements its designs with vintage works from the twentieth century and well-edited home goods sourced from local artisans. Find limited-release bowls and vases from native Angeleno Victoria Morris, lamps from Beth Katz of Mt. Washington Pottery, minimalist sculptures from Pasadena-based Carol Horst Ceramics, and more.

12. OK

8303 West 3rd Street,
West Hollywood

One of the best gift stores in Los Angeles sits on Third Street near West Hollywood, a well-to-do area known for its concentration of restaurants and furniture and design stores. Owned and expertly edited by Larry Schaffer, it's a go-to desti-nation for those interested in housewares, books, and jewelry with a modernist bent. Think cast-iron mor-tars and pestles, Japanese cocktail shakers, and copper kitchen timers. Find additional locations in Santa Monica and Silver Lake.

13. Standing's Butchery

7016 Melrose Avenue,
Hollywood

Angelenos who care about ethically sourced and sustainably raised meat and poultry turn to butcher Jered Standing. At his Hollywood butcher shop, Standing guides shop-pers toward lesser-known cuts and provides cooking advice if needed. In addition to house-made meatballs, sausages, and duck and chicken confit, the shop carries a solid selection of pantry items, from dried beans to pasta and kimchi.

14. TableArt

Pacific Design Center,
Green Building,
700 N San Vicente Boulevard,
West Hollywood

TableArt is a must-visit for serious home enter-tainers who care as much about tablescapes as what's served on the plate. Walter Lowry stocks his 3,400-square-foot store, which opened on Melrose Avenue a decade ago, with exquisite tabletop furnish-ings, including handmade or mouth-blown glassware, linens, and dinnerware featuring hand-painted or handmade patterns.

15. The Original Farmers Market

6333 West 3rd Street, Beverly Grove

The Original Farmers Market was founded in the summer of 1934 when a group of local farmers pulled their pickup trucks into an empty lot at the corner of Third and Fairfax and began selling fresh fruits, vegetables, and flowers to passersby. In the nearly ninety years since its inception, the dirt lot has evolved into a year-round marketplace with a dizzying selection of artisanal food stalls, restaurants, and produce vendors. The exceptional retailers that call the market home include Littlejohn's English Toffee and Monsieur Marcel Gourmet Market, a destination for fancy cheeses and artisanal food products.

16. Slammers Cafe at Brain Dead Studios

611 North Fairfax Avenue, Fairfax

Swing into Slammers Cafe, located in the back garden at the art house cinema Brain Dead Studios for coffee, small bites, and one-of-a-kind pantry items. The daytime menu features locally sourced rice bowls, salads, and sandwiches, while the all-day espresso bar brews single-origin coffee from local roastery Heavy Water. Available to go is a fun line of food collaborations, including green olive oil from Vecere Abruzzo, a mole spice mix from Sunset Cultures, and a pancake mix from Hollywood's Clark Street Diner (page 89).

17. Vromage

7988 Sunset Boulevard, West Hollywood

Find Los Angeles's first dairy-free cheese shop tucked into the hills of West Hollywood. At Vromage, founder Youssef Fahouri delights vegan cheese lovers with a seasonal selection available for nibbling on-site with fruits and nuts or packaged to go for later. Also on the menu are salads and open-faced sandwiches that highlight the store's line of cheeses.

BEYOND RESTAURANTS

Coffee Shops:
Alfred Coffee
Dialog Café
Paramount Coffee
   Project

Bars:
The Abbey
Employees Only
Jumbo's Clown Room
Tabula Rasa Bar

Bakeries:
Diamond Bakery
Sweet Lady Jane

Ice Cream:
Awan
Dear Bella Creamery
Happy Ice
Mashti Malone's

LA ICONS

By Hillary Dixler Canavan

In a city dismissed as ruinously obsessed with the new, young, and beautiful, LA's roster of bona fide restaurant icons reveals something far truer: This is a place that is fiercely loyal to what makes it great.

These legendary spots are part of the fabric of life in LA, and locals and visitors alike shouldn't miss the chance to explore the history on these tables. There's a reason the city keeps coming back to these icons.

OLD HOLLYWOOD

These are the multi-decade haunts where the city's culture makers, stars, and power players have plotted and partied for generations. *Listed in chronological order, from oldest to youngest.*

The Musso & Frank Grill

6667 Hollywood Boulevard, Hollywood

The first and final name in all things Old Hollywood, this century-old bastion of LA fine dining (page 20), which opened in 1919, still delivers epic night-out vibes and a hell of a good martini. Keep it classic with an avocado cocktail and a steak or one of the daily specials (like the Thursday potpie).

Tam O'Shanter

2980 Los Feliz Boulevard, Atwater Village

Occupying the same Tudor-style building in Atwater Village since 1922, Tam O'Shanter was famously one of Walt Disney's haunts. Ask for table thirty-one if you want to sit where the OG imagineer sat while you dig into excellent prime rib, Yorkshire pudding, and mashed potatoes.

The Prince

31980½ West 7th Street, Koreatown

This classic Koreatown restaurant (page 64) began life in the 1940s as the Windsor, attracting a Hollywood clientele and directors' eyes: Its sultry red interior has been in everything from *Chinatown* to *Mad Men*. New ownership in the 1990s transformed the restaurant into what it is today: an absurdly fun place to dig into Korean fried chicken.

The Dresden

1760 North Vermont Avenue, Los Feliz

Famous on-screen (see: *Swingers*) and off-, this 1954 landmark with both a formal dining room and a more casual lounge is known for live music, classic cocktails (order a Blood & Sand), and its dark Hollywood charm.

Casa Vega

13301 Ventura Boulevard, Sherman Oaks

The Valley isn't Hollywood, but Hollywood has been dining in the Valley since the midfifties thanks to Casa Vega, still run by the Vega family. The menu of Mexican hits includes tableside guacamole, tamales, churros, and, of course, margaritas.

Dan Tana's

9071 Santa Monica Boulevard, West Hollywood

This bastion of pasta, parm, and panache, which opened in 1964 (page 90), still boasts a celebrity clientele today, even after fifty-plus years in business. Try the giant veal parm and let the Chianti flow.

Spago

176 North Canon Drive, Beverly Hills

About twenty years after Dan Tana's opened—in 1982, to be exact—Wolfgang Puck remade the LA restaurant scene with his celebrity and paparazzi magnet Spago (page 115), which in the present day still bustles with both locals and visitors alike. Don't forget to order the pizza topped with smoked salmon and caviar, perhaps his most famous dish since the early 1980s.

5 ICONIC LA DISHES

Movie stars aren't the only celebrities in this town. From loaded sandwiches to perfect burgers to spicy grilled snook, here are five dishes worth their own walk of fame. *Listed in chronological order.*

Beef Double Dip— Philippe The Original
1001 North Alameda Street, Chinatown

The invention of the French dip is widely credited to this 1908-founded restaurant (page 69), and the most popular order on the menu these days is the beef double dip: a roast beef sandwich on French bread, dipped in the jus from the roasting process. "Double dip" means both the top and the bottom halves of the sandwich are soaked in jus. Note that both cheese and mustard are optional.

Hickory Burger—The Apple Pan
10801 West Pico Boulevard, West LA

When you sidle up to the vintage counter at the Apple Pan (page 113), you owe it to yourself to order its quintessential 1940s menu item. The hickory burger is a thing of simple beauty: a well-griddled patty topped with melted cheddar, lettuce, and the eponymous, proprietary hickory barbecue sauce.

The #19— Langer's Delicatessen-Restaurant
704 South Alvarado Street, MacArthur Park

This sandwich features hand-sliced pastrami—made using the restaurant's original 1940s-era recipe—topped with Swiss cheese and coleslaw between two slices of rye bread, sourced for decades from Fred's Bakery & Deli. Not only is it easily the best deli in LA, but plenty of Angelenos will also tell you this pastrami sandwich rivals any from Katz's in New York City.

Slippery Shrimp—Yang Chow

819 North Broadway, Chinatown

Standing proud in the heart of Chinatown since 1977, Yang Chow (page 71) is most famous for its slippery shrimp: The fried shrimp are coated in an instantly familiar sweet and sticky chili sauce. The dining room feels preserved in amber, too, with wall-to-wall maroon carpet, white tablecloths, and pink cloth napkins.

Pescado Zaradeado—Coni'Seafood

3544 West Imperial Highway, Inglewood

Some version of this grilled, butterflied snook—emblematic of Nayarit-style Mexican cooking—has been available courtesy of the Cossio family since the eighties (page 127). These days, second-generation chef Connie Cossio carries on the family tradition. The mild, white-fleshed fish is slicked with house sauce and served with raw red onions, cucumber slices, and tortillas. Wrap a little fish and onion in a tortilla and go to town.

TRIED-AND-TRUE INSTITUTIONS

Everything on this list of stalwarts opened before 2000, and this collection only scratches the surface. This being Los Angeles, our institutions include everything from a seaside fried-fish joint to sit-down Mexican restaurants to temples of sushi. *Listed in chronological order.*

Cielito Lindo

23 Olvera Street, Downtown

Cielito Lindo has been slinging beef taquitos in avocado salsa since 1934. It's a true taste of LA's Chicano history, right at the edge of Chinatown.

Otomisan

2506½ 1st Street, Boyle Heights

Back in the fifties, Boyle Heights was home to an enclave of Japanese Americans. While the neighborhood has changed, Otomisan (page 37) has continued serving well-executed Japanese comfort fare like tempura, udon, pork katsu curry, and oyakodon since 1956.

Neptune's Net
42505 Pacific Coast Highway, Malibu

No trip to Malibu is complete without the fried seafood from this fifties-era seafood shack. Most customers opt for a seafood sampler or fish and chips.

Pie 'n Burger
913 East California Boulevard, Pasadena

In charming Pasadena, this sixties ode to Formica and soda fountains (page 14) still turns out killer burgers, impressively large slices of pie, and fine diner fare.

Harold & Belle's
2920 West Jefferson Boulevard, Jefferson Park

Now run by third-generation owners, Harold & Belle's (page 128) brings New Orleans charm to the Crenshaw neighborhood with a menu of hits like po' boys, gumbo, and étouffée.

Jitlada
5233 Sunset Boulevard, East Hollywood

Perhaps the best-known restaurant in Thai Town, Jitlada was already more than thirty years old when a review by legendary critic Jonathan Gold shot the restaurant into the stratosphere.

Michael's
1147 3rd Street, Santa Monica

Sometimes credited as the birthplace of California cuisine, Michael's has attracted big-name chefs and adoring diners since it opened in 1979. The restaurant also famously boasts an amazing collection of modern art.

Sushi Gen
422 East 2nd Street, Little Tokyo

Sushi's journey from Japanese import to widespread availability in America really kicked off in Los Angeles (page 134), where restaurants like Sushi Gen treated the cuisine with the care it deserves. Head to this long-standing Little Tokyo spot for the well-priced sashimi lunch special, or treat yourself for a more expansive meal at the perpetually packed counter.

Golden Deli
815 West Las Tunas Drive, San Gabriel

The San Gabriel Valley isn't just home to the city's finest Chinese cooking: Since 1981, it's also been home to some of the best

Vietnamese food. Golden Deli (page 12) is best known for its cha gio, egg rolls that are deep-fried to crispy perfection, but trust that the expansive menu is full of hits, including pho, bun, and banh mi.

Dai Ho Restaurant
9148 Las Tunas Drive, Temple City

This institution (page 12), which originally opened in Alhambra but moved to neighboring Temple City in 1998, has been serving up its legendary Taiwanese-style beef soup in the SGV since the 1980s. The undisputed star is the noodles: bouncy and a fine example of "Q," or the ideal chewiness associated with fish balls, boba, and the like.

Guelaguetza
3014 West Olympic Boulevard, Koreatown

A beacon of color and mole in the heart of Koreatown, Guelaguetza has been lauded as one of the city's finest Mexican restaurants since the Lopez family opened its doors in the mid-1990s. Along with the famous mole, there is a beloved selection of tlayudas (a wide tortilla slathered with unrefined lard and other toppings, then grilled), tamales, meats, and empanadas.

BCD Tofu House
3575 Wilshire Boulevard, Koreatown

Now a slick mini chain, BCD Tofu House began life in 1996 as a soondubu (soft tofu stew) specialist on Vermont Avenue in Koreatown. The third location on Wilshire (opened in 2000) is the most recognizable, and the one we're recommending: It's open well into the wee morning hours.

Birrieria Nochistlán
3200 East 4th Street, Boyle Heights

When the late Silverio Moreno and his wife, Amparo Luis Bustos, started selling birria from their home in the late 1990s, they had no idea that by 2021 birria would become one of the most popular Mexican dishes in the country. Their business grew and changed as the decades passed, but Birrieria Nochistlán (page 35), now under the care of the couple's daughter, is still turning out some of the city's best goat stew.

La Casita Mexicana
4030 East Gage Avenue, Bell

Southeast of Los Angeles in the smaller city of Bell, La Casita Mexicana has enjoyed its reputation as one of the region's loveliest sit-down Mexican restaurants since it opened back in 1998. The menu pulls from Jalisco, and the chef-owners, Jaime Martin del Campo and Ramiro Arvizu, have become celebrities in their own right, frequently appearing on Univision.

NEXT-GEN LEGENDS

These are the restaurants that have opened since 2000 that are poised for multi-decade dominance; they've already shaped LA restaurant culture tremendously. *Listed in chronological order.*

Father's Office

1018 Montana Avenue, Santa Monica

When chef Sang Yoon took over his favorite Santa Monica bar in 2000, he gifted LA with one of its most iconic dishes—a dry-aged beef patty topped with bacon, arugula, Gruyère, blue cheese, bacon-caramelized onions, and never ketchup—and was at the forefront of America's infatuation with gastropubs. Even today, with two more Father's Office (page 146) locations around town, the burger is still epically popular and epically divisive.

Sea Harbour

3939 Rosemead Boulevard, Rosemead

Chef Tony He earned his moniker as LA's godfather of dim sum with Sea Harbour, which has reigned as one of the region's finest dim sum parlors since opening in 2001. He famously eschews dim sum carts and claims credit for inventing modern dim sum dishes now popular worldwide, like truffle-sauce-topped har gow. (Also try his cooking at Chef Tony, page 11.)

A.O.C.

8700 West 3rd Street, West Hollywood

Part wine bar, part Mediterranean small-plates restaurant, part absolutely dreamy patio destination, A.O.C. (page 89) feels like a new restaurant, not one that's more than twenty years old. Chef Suzanne Goin and restaurateur-somm Caroline Styne weren't just pioneers; they were predictors.

Parks BBQ

955 South Vermont Avenue G, Koreatown

Known for its high-end prime, Kobe, and Wagyu beef cuts, Parks BBQ (page 69) quickly won fans for its vision of soigné Korean barbecue. The rest of the menu wows, too, with expert banchan and impressive traditional dishes.

Mozza

641 North Highland Avenue, Hollywood; 6602 Melrose Avenue, Hollywood

Nancy Silverton was already one of the biggest names in LA food when she opened Pizzeria Mozza in 2007 and its sibling Osteria Mozza a few months later. Laying claim to some of the city's most outstanding pizza, delicious desserts (seriously, the butterscotch budino), and high-end Italian cooking all in one building is all the more impressive for still being true more than fifteen years in.

Gjelina
1429 Abbot Kinney Boulevard, Venice

Gjelina opened in 2008, remaking local and visitors' understanding of Venice and Abbot Kinney Boulevard along with it. Beautifully chic diners still clamor to dig into creatively topped pizzas and small plates that lean heavily on amazing local produce and house charcuterie.

Kogi
Mutliple locations

Los Angeles couldn't have asked for a better evangelist for its collision of culinary cultures *and* its robust street food scene than Roy Choi, who changed the game when he started telling Twitter where he'd park his Kogi truck that day. His Korean short rib tacos were as much an instant icon as the story itself, the stuff of true LA legend.

Leo's Tacos
Multiple locations

Leo's Tacos went from a single, al pastor–focused taco truck in 2010 to a veritable fleet, covering nine locations today. Along with tacos, the trucks make killer mulitas, tortas, and nachos.

Night + Market
9043 Sunset Boulevard West, West Hollywood

In 2011, chef Kris Yenbamroong took over his parents' neighborhood Thai restaurant, and LA dining hasn't been the same since. Expert Thai cooking, a best-in-town natural wine list, and all the party vibes are signatures of the now-multiple Night + Market locations (see also page 91).

Chengdu Taste
828 West Valley Boulevard, Alhambra

In ten short years, Chengdu Taste (page 11) went from new SGV restaurant to the SGV's crown jewel to a mini chain with locations as far-flung as Honolulu and Seattle. That's the power of amazing Sichuan cooking and beloved dishes like toothpick lamb with cumin, boiled fish with green pepper sauce, and god-tier mapo tofu.

Check out **Eater LA's classics map** for an evolving look at the icons we're especially excited about right now:

HOTELS WITH THE BEST FOOD BUILT IN

By Martha Cheng

In recent years, LA's hotel restaurants have attracted celebrity chefs near and far, making the hotel dining rooms destinations in themselves, both for the food and for the often stunning design and rooftop vistas.

Beverly Wilshire

9500 Wilshire Boulevard, Beverly Hills

Inside the Four Seasons, the flagship location of CUT (page 113) by Wolfgang Puck remains one of the city's best steakhouses, where minimalist luxury meets steaks grilled over wood and charcoal and finished in a 1200-degree broiler.

Downtown LA Proper Hotel

1100 South Broadway, Downtown

James Beard Award winners Suzanne Goin and Caroline Styne (Lucques, AOC) have you covered from morning to midnight, breakfast to booze, at their three spots: the rooftop Cara Cara, Portuguese-influenced Caldo Verde, and intimate bar Dahlia.

Freehand Hotel

416 West 8th Street, Downtown

At the Exchange, Israeli and Southeast Asian flavors mingle, while on the rooftop, Miami export Broken Shaker serves cocktails poolside.

Fairmont Miramar

101 Wilshire Boulevard, Santa Monica

Less like a hotel restaurant than a California bistro, Fig at the Fairmont sources from the nearby Santa Monica farmers market for its sunny Mediterranean dishes. Get there right on time for happy hour from 5 to 6 P.M., when almost everything on the menu is half off.

Hotel Covell

4626 Hollywood Boulevard, Los Feliz

Start at Bar Covell, a destination wine bar where in lieu of drinks menus, knowledgeable bartenders guide you through the bottles and taps; get room service from Tex-Mex spot HomeState downstairs; and for the morning after, grab coffee at Go Get Em Tiger next door.

Hotel Normandie

605 South Normandie Avenue, Koreatown

Satisfy diner cravings at Cassell's Hamburgers, with its legendary patty melt, and fine-dining leanings at Le Comptoir's ten-seat counter and vegetable tasting menu.

The Hoxton
1060 South Broadway, Downtown

Hospitality giant Boka Restaurant Group operates the restaurants at this Downtown hotel, which include Stephanie Izard's Peruvian restaurant Cabra.

Line Hotel
3515 Wilshire Boulevard, Koreatown

At Openaire, inside a lush greenhouse, LA restaurant veteran Josiah Citrin offers up modern American flavors that skirt the edge between formal and casual.

Maybourne Beverly Hills
225 North Canon Drive, Beverly Hills

New York City institution Dante serves up aperitivi and Italian flavors to transport you from one sunwashed destination (an LA rooftop) to another (the Italian coast).

The Shay
8801 Washington Boulevard, Culver City

The West Coast outpost of Etta, from Chicago, focuses on vegetables and meats passed through a wood-fired hearth alongside pizza and pasta.

Silver Lake Pool & Inn
4141 Santa Monica Boulevard, Silver Lake

Poolside Italian hotel restaurants are practically a cliché in Los Angeles, but Marco Polo at this boutique hotel keeps it relaxed in vibes and in its menu, centered on restrained antipasti and pasta.

Tommie Hollywood
6516 Selma Avenue, Hollywood

Ka'teen imports the Yucatán to Hollywood via a five-thousand-square-foot jungle oasis of outdoor dining and a menu by star chef Wes Avila.

Beverly Hills
Sawtelle
West LA
Westwood

BEVERL

TO WI

5

Y HILLS

EST LA

BEVERLY HILLS TO WEST LA

DINING

1. The Apple Pan
2. Avra Beverly Hills
3. Big Boi Filipino
4. Crustacean
5. CUT
6. Emporium Thai
7. Hamasaku
8. Hermanito
9. John O' Groats
10. Lamonica's NY Pizza
11. Matū
12. Maude
13. Mogu Mogu
14. Monte Alban Restaurant
15. Nanbankan
16. Nate'n Al's
17. Nozawa Bar
18. Sonoritas Prime Tacos
19. Spago
20. Taste of Tehran
21. Tempura House
22. Tsujita LA Artisan Noodle Annex
23. Tuk Tuk Thai
24. Yakitoriya
25. Yazawa

SHOPPING

1. Attari
2. The Cheese Store of Beverly Hills
3. Edelweiss Chocolates
4. European Deluxe Sausage Kitchen
5. K Chocolatier by Diane Krön

BEVERLY HILLS TO WEST LA
DINING

West LA hasn't always been considered the most vibrant dining neighborhood in the city, but it's more than worth a visit. The area known as Sawtelle is a local destination for all sorts of Asian food; the concentrated blocks of Sawtelle Boulevard between Santa Monica and Olympic Sawtelle Boulevard are lined with countless Japanese, Korean, and Thai restaurants (many with patrons lined up to get in).

Westwood, while mostly known as the home of UCLA, is where you'll find Tehrangeles and some of the best Persian food in the city, as well as shop-lined streets and plenty of mom-and-pop gems.

On the other end of the spectrum, there's affluent fine-dining mecca Beverly Hills, home of Rodeo Drive, landmarks like the Beverly Hills Hotel, wide streets lined with mansions, and the most high-end fashion boutiques in the city. There, where luxury labels abound, the restaurants are as upscale as they are impressive in stature—but there are also more approachable places in the 90210 zip code if you know where to look.

1. The Apple Pan

10801 West Pico Boulevard, West LA

A much-beloved Westside institution known for its hickory burger (page 138), layered with a crunchy wedge of lettuce that's bigger than your head and served in a humble diner-like stand along Pico Boulevard, the Apple Pan makes consistently good sandwiches and pies. It's hard to think of a more enduring greasy spoon in LA. The counter is small, so be prepared for a wait.

2. Avra Beverly Hills

233 North Beverly Drive, Beverly Hills

New York City import Avra serves up modern Greek fare in the heart of the Golden Triangle (the area between Santa Monica Boulevard, Wilshire Boulevard, and Canon Drive). The emphasis at this neutral-toned stunner is on pristine seafood that's beautifully displayed for guests to select their ideal catch. Load up on the stellar appetizers, too, like grilled prawns, feta-tomato salad, and comforting manouri saganaki, phyllo dough stuffed with manouri cheese laced with sweet honey and balsamic glaze.

3. Big Boi Filipino

2027 Sawtelle Boulevard, Sawtelle

Chef-owner Barb Batiste opened Big Boi to honor her late father, and her compact, casual homestyle restaurant on Sawtelle dazzles with modern takes on classic Filipino dishes. As one of LA's early successful modern Filipino upstarts, Big Boi serves favorites like chicken adobo, beef giniling, lumpia (fried spring rolls, shown opposite), and sisig, plus pancit and garlic rice on the side.

4. Crustacean

468 North Bedford Drive, Beverly Hills

Modern Vietnamese fare by chef Helene An is what it is all about at the long-standing Crustacean in Beverly Hills, a two-floor corner restaurant outfitted with white tablecloths and plush seating. Don't sleep on the famous garlic noodles or the garlic-roasted Dungeness crab served in or out of its shell—go big and get both.

5. CUT

9500 Wilshire Boulevard, Beverly Hills

Located on the ground floor of the ritzy Beverly Wilshire hotel, this modern steakhouse from Wolfgang Puck serves high-quality red meat ranging from bone-in USDA Prime beef rib eye to A5 Wagyu filet mignon with chef-driven flourishes like the bone marrow flan starter. Save room for the chocolate soufflé for dessert.

6. Emporium Thai

1275 Westwood Boulevard, Westwood

Westwood's stalwart Thai spot Emporium draws on the deep roots that owner John Sungkamee and chef Gina Sungkamee have in southern Thailand. The menu at the colorful restaurant draws from across the country, though of course the spicy southern dishes are the highlights here. The curry-laced Phuket wings, crying beef salad, and Jitlada-style green curry mussels (shown above; for Jitlada, see page 102) are must-orders.

7. Hamasaku

11043 Santa Monica Boulevard, Sawtelle

In a space just off bustling Sawtelle, Hamasaku's understated elegance, use of local ingredients, excellent omakase, and beautiful bar make it a draw for expense-account and celebratory dinners. The best place to observe the chef in action is the L-shaped sushi bar, so be sure to reserve a spot there.

8. Hermanito

2024 Sawtelle Boulevard, Sawtelle

Bar Hermanito is one of the most surprising—and satisfying—dining choices on Sawtelle. The menu takes inspiration from the neighborhood's Sawtelle Japantown culture and history with inflections of Mexican dishes like yellowtail tostada with Japanese pickles. The best reasons to come to Hermanito, though, are its tacos, smooth cocktails, and Westside-cool patio atmosphere. More common choices like quesabirria tacos are complemented by a Beijing duck platter (check for availability).

9. John O'Groats

10516 West Pico Boulevard, West LA

John O'Groats is one of those LA legends to love. Robert and Angelica Jacoby opened this lunch and breakfast standby in 1982, serving food only during daytime hours so they could care for their sons after school. Robert passed away in 2018, but they're still making the beloved biscuits, pancakes, eggs, and sandwiches that keep people coming in.

10. Lamonica's NY Pizza

1066 Gayley Avenue, Westwood

The UCLA crowd and Westwood locals know what's up with Lamonica's, a New York–style slice shop that's been in business for over forty years. They even import their fresh dough from Brooklyn (something about the water)—that's how dedicated they are. Grab a slice of pepperoni, a garlic knot, and a table and have yourself an NYC experience in LA.

11. Matū

239 South Beverly Drive, Beverly Hills

Featuring only New Zealand–raised, grass-fed Wagyu beef from First Light Farms, Matū is a dimly lit, impressively sleek steak-focused restaurant in the heart of Beverly Hills. Most diners opt for the reasonably priced tasting menu. Of course, there's wood-grilled steak, but starters might include arugula-laced carpaccio or braised beef croquetas.

12. Maude

212 South Beverly Drive, Beverly Hills

After more than a decade, Curtis Stone's Beverly Hills tasting-menu restaurant has become an enduring essential in Los Angeles. Stone and chef de cuisine Osiel Gastelum execute seasonally changing nine-course dinners with wine pairings in a twenty-four-seat jewel box decked out in opulent royal-blue tones and gold accents. Stone's Hollywood steak house, Gwen, is also worth a trip.

13. Mogu Mogu

11555 West Olympic Boulevard, West LA

A small shop specializing in mazemen (broth-free ramen), Mogu Mogu loads everything from spicy minced pork to chashu to poached eggs to vegetables atop its silky noodles. The key with mazemen is to mix everything together, so select a combo and then get stirring for the ultimate experience.

14. Monte Alban Restaurant

11929 Santa Monica Boulevard, West LA

Best known for its homemade moles, Oaxacan restaurant Monte Alban has been a draw in West LA for more than twenty-five years. Tucked into a strip mall, it serves tlayudas and moles paired with rice molded into the shape of a pyramid, alongside flashy molcajetes full of roasted meats, cheese, and vegetables partially submerged in bubbling salsa.

15. Nanbankan
11330 Santa Monica Boulevard, Sawtelle

This brightly lit, affordable yakitori (grilled meat) spot writes its daily specials on a marker board. Pair the fantastic tsukune (chicken meatballs) with one of the restaurant's draft sakes. To make sure you get to try the most popular skewers, which are cooked on two large robata grills behind the bar, it's best to arrive early, before the restaurant sells out.

16. Nate'n Al's
414 North Beverly Drive, Beverly Hills

This iconic Beverly Hills deli serves reliably good, overstuffed pastrami and corned beef sandwiches in its no-fuss dining room outfitted with brown leather booths. Their extensive breakfast offerings, including cheese blintzes, matzo brei, and plenty of smoked fishes, are also worth checking out.

17. Nozawa Bar
212 North Canon Drive, Beverly Hills

A sister restaurant of the popular local sushi mini chain Sugarfish, this secret high-end sushi bar is tucked behind the Beverly Hills Sugarfish. It's overseen by chef Osamu Fujita, who prepares a seasonal, market-driven menu that stands up to similarly priced places in Tokyo. Unlike with Sugarfish, reservations for this intimate find are required.

18. Sonoritas Prime Tacos
2004 Sawtelle Boulevard, Sawtelle

Sawtelle is not the first place one thinks of for great tacos. But Sonoritas prepares some of the best carne asada using actual steak cuts instead of chopped-up odds and ends, something one would see in Mexicali and other places in Sonora. So yes, when someone wants great carne asada, this is the first place to look.

19. Spago
176 North Canon Drive, Beverly Hills

With a fancy bar near the front for cocktails and small bites and a main dining room dedicated to tasting menus and à la carte options, there's something for everyone at Wolfgang Puck's still-buzzing flagship restaurant in Beverly Hills. Don't be surprised to see Puck roaming the dining room and kitchen most nights of the week.

20. Taste of Tehran
1915 Westwood Boulevard, Westwood

A meal at casual West LA staple Taste of Tehran is as close as it gets to a meal at a Persian grandma's home. The ghormeh sabzi stew (a beef-and-bean stew punctuated by herbs like fenugreek) is as nourishing and soul-warming as restaurant food comes, and the kebab plates adorned with grilled tomato are exactly what on-the-go locals grab for weekday lunches.

21. Tempura House
1816 Sawtelle Boulevard, Sawtelle

Just a few blocks north of the main drag of Sawtelle, the classic Tempura House serves reasonably priced bento of homestyle Japanese fare, with protein options ranging from deep-fried chicken katsu cutlets and mench katsu (fried hamburg steak) to the restaurant's namesake fried shrimp. Open since 1949, it's one of LA's oldest Japanese restaurants.

22. Tsujita LA Artisan Noodle Annex

2050 Sawtelle Boulevard, Sawtelle

Located across the street from Sawtelle's Tsujita, one of the undeniable favorites for ramen in the city, the Annex location has become just as popular as the original. With thicker noodles and an ultra-rich broth that's chock-full of garlic and pork back fat, this isn't a noodle soup for the faint of heart. The dippable tsukemen (shown above) is tinged with a vinegary kick and is always a good bet.

23. Tuk Tuk Thai

1638 Sawtelle Boulevard, Sawtelle

The family from a long-standing Thai restaurant on Fairfax opened Tuk Tuk Thai with a mostly street-food menu on Sawtelle in early 2022. Find classic dishes like Isaan sour sausage and prik khing moo grob (stir-fried pork belly tinged with red chiles) in the small-but-cozy space decorated with light pink walls. There's a handy patio, too, for street-side alfresco dining.

24. Yakitoriya

11301 West Olympic Boulevard, Sawtelle

The namesake dish at this Sawtelle staple comes in enough varieties to please everyone. Yakitori beginners can start with the popular chicken thighs before graduating to options like gizzards and hearts, all grilled over binchotan. Sidle up to the long light-wood bar, or grab a stool at one of the low tables, and enjoy delicious things grilled on sticks.

25. Yazawa

9669 South Santa Monica Boulevard, Beverly Hills

Offering one of the best yakiniku (tabletop grilled meat) experiences in LA, upscale Japanese barbecue restaurant Yazawa obsesses over meat sourcing and imports their selections directly from Japan. Because it's in Beverly Hills, the dining room has some fancy flourishes, like leather booths and elegant chandeliers.

QR CODES

for our online guides to these neighborhoods:

BEVERLY HILLS

SAWTELLE

WESTWOOD

BEVERLY HILLS TO WEST LA
SHOPPING

Find an interesting mix of shopping possibilities from Beverly Hills to West LA. Catering to well-heeled neighbors, along with UCLA's student body, the neighborhoods of Sawtelle, Westwood, and Beverly Hills have something for every budget, offering high-end boutiques, quirky independently owned shops, and everything in between.

1. Attari
1388 Westwood Boulevard, Westwood

Attari is one of the longest-standing Persian businesses lining the stretch of Westwood Boulevard between Olympic and Wilshire in an area known as Tehrangeles. In addition to hefty baguette sandwiches filled with tongue and herbaceous seasonal soups, the shop carries plenty of prepared foods ideal for a Persian picnic. Grab some yogurt drinks, freshly made salads, sandwiches, and baklava—all to go.

2. The Cheese Store of Beverly Hills
9705 South Santa Monica Boulevard, Beverly Hills

While specialty stores dedicated to selling cheese are commonplace today, back in 1967, when Colonel Sigmund Roth opened the Cheese Store of Beverly Hills, it was one of the first in the country. The abundantly stocked shop sells an incredible variety of cheese, as well as gourmet products like truffles, caviar, and charcuterie. Today the store is owned by twenty-year employee Dominick DiBartolomeo, who continues the store's long tradition of introducing and delighting shoppers with rare cheeses.

3. Edelweiss Chocolates
444 North Canon Drive, Beverly Hills

Chocolate lovers have been lining up at Edelweiss Chocolates since 1942. The shop is particularly famous for its chocolate-dipped treats, including marshmallows in flavors like mocha and mint, candied fruits like peach and pineapple, and an array of bonbons filled with raspberry and maple creams. The chocolate-covered pretzels and Oreos are easy crowd-pleasers. The prices are high, but the freshness and quality are excellent at this stalwart shop.

4. European Deluxe Sausage Kitchen
9109 West Olympic Boulevard, Beverly Hills

Amid luxury storefronts like Gucci and Louis Vuitton, find a gourmet butcher shop specializing in scratch-made German, Italian, and Polish sausages, as well as South African jerky (biltong), since 1948.

5. K Chocolatier by Diane Krön
9606 Santa Monica Boulevard, Beverly Hills

Diane and Tom Krön have been in the chocolate game since the 1970s under the Krön Chocolatier brand and are well-known for their chocolate-covered strawberries and Budapest crème truffles made of just whipped cream, cocoa, rum, and dark chocolate. The couple opened K Chocolatier in Beverly Hills more than two decades ago, specializing in handmade chocolates inspired by age-old family recipes dating back to four generations of Hungarian chocolate makers. Find an additional location of K Chocolatier in Malibu.

BEYOND RESTAURANTS

Coffee Shops:
10 Speed Coffee
C+M
Coffee Tomo
Fountain Coffee Room

Bars:
Nic's on Beverly
Plan Check Kitchen
    + Bar
Thunderbird Bar
The Wellesbourne

Bakeries:
Amandine Patisserie
    Café
Artelice Pâtisserie
B Sweet Dessert Bar
Chaumont Bakery &
    Café

Ice Cream:
Honeymee
Saffron & Rose
SomiSomi
Wanderlust Creamery

SPOTLIGHT: THE VALLEY

DINING

LA's San Fernando Valley is so much more than the lilting accent that has so long stereotyped it. The swath of land just north of the LA basin is a multicultural hub that sneakily includes some of the region's best, most diverse eats and specialty shops, many buried in strip-malls along the famed Ventura Boulevard.

Anajak Thai
14704 Ventura Boulevard, Sherman Oaks
The James Beard Award–winning Thai restaurant is a must-visit for its elaborate tasting menus as well as its industry-heavy Taco Tuesdays.

Bill's Burgers
14742 Oxnard Street, Van Nuys
A valley legend, this simple burger stand serves up stellar versions of the California classic.

Borekas Sephardic Pastries
15030 Ventura Boulevard, Sherman Oaks
Flaky, stuffed Israeli phyllo pastries are what draw lines of fans each morning to this Sherman Oaks strip mall storefront.

Brent's Deli
19565 Parthenia Street, Northridge
Brent's in Northridge is a half-century-old institution for a reason. Try the usuals like pastrami and corned beef piled high on rye.

The Brothers Sushi
21418 Ventura Boulevard, Woodland Hills
You can go a la carte or omakase at this Woodland Hills sushi haven (page 134); either way you won't be disappointed.

Casa Vega
13301 Ventura Boulevard, Sherman Oaks
This family-owned staple (page 99) blends celebrity-magnet with neighborhood-fave vibes with its expansive Mexican menu and upbeat party energy.

Gasolina
21150 Ventura Boulevard, Woodland Hills
A Spanish gem tucked in Woodland Hills gives the Valley communities their fix of pan con tomate, tortilla española, and monthly paellas.

Go's Mart
22330 Sherman Way, Canoga Park
Sushi connoisseurs love to name-drop this hidden strip-mall gem in off-the-radar Canoga Park, where Go-San wows regulars with his stellar if occasionally unconventional sushi creations.

Kobee Factory
14110 Oxnard Street, Van Nuys
Yet another Valley strip mall houses some of the region's finest Syrian delights, from shawarma and falafel to braised lamb shank and the namesake kobee—pointed meat and bulgur meatballs fried to a crisp golden brown.

Petit Trois
13705 Ventura Boulevard, Sherman Oaks
In one of the first LA-based high-end restaurants to expand into the Valley, Ludo Lefebvre French fare (page 139) is just as good in its larger dining room in Sherman Oaks.

Porto's Bakery
315 North Brand Boulevard, Glendale
No LA party is complete without a big yellow box of pastries from the region's most beloved Cuban bakery. Come for cheese rolls, potato balls, empanadas, guava cakes, and more.

Sadaf
16240 Ventura Boulevard, Encino
Sadaf, with locations in Encino and Thousand Oaks, serves the Valley's huge Persian population upscale Iranian delights from their homeland.

Topanga Social
6600 CA-27, Canoga Park
Some of LA's most viral food sensations converge in this shopping-mall food hall, where far west Valley residents can come for wildly creative burgers, donuts, drinks, dumplings, and so much more.

SHOPPING

Epicurus Gourmet
12140 Sherman Way, North Hollywood
Get lost at Epicurus Gourmet, a specialty food distributor and wholesaler that stocks more than two thousand high-end products from Europe and across the globe. Though the warehouse ambience leaves something to be desired, this hidden gem is popular among culinary professionals and the food-loving public for rare condiments, vinegars, butter, jams, chocolate, and more.

Erewhon
12833 Ventura Boulevard, Studio City
Make sure to pencil in an entire afternoon for shopping at this bastion for bleeding-edge health and wellness food products, including plant-based protein powders, jarred sea moss, and mushroom tinctures. Also on-site is a café selling sandwiches, sushi, and pizza, as well as a tonic bar hawking smoothies, açai bowls, and bone broth, alongside coffee and matcha tea beverages. Erewhon has a total of seven locations in Los Angeles, including stores in Silver Lake, Venice, and Santa Monica.

Furn Saj
11146 Balboa Boulevard, Granada Hills
After polishing off one of the best shawarmas in all of Los Angeles at this Lebanese bakery, check out the display case filled with sweet and savory baked goods for something later. The flatbreads dusted with za'atar spice or slathered with spicy tomato-onion jam reheat especially well, along with the cheese saroukh, a sesame seed–studded bread filled with cheese, onions,

spices, and parsley. Rice pudding and custard in the cold display case make for a sweet finish.

The Joint
13718 Ventura Boulevard, Sherman Oaks
This seafood market/café specializes in sustainably sourced, dry-aged seafood. Some locals swing by for filets of salmon or yellowtail for dinner; others linger around enjoying coffees, pastries, and sandwiches. While it's unusual for a daytime spot to share real estate with a fish market, the brightly lit and airy space just works somehow.

Studio City Farmers Market
2052 Ventura Place, Studio City
Held on Saturdays from eight A.M. to one P.M., the Studio City Farmers Market is equal parts quaint and delicious. Amid the bounty of seasonal vegetables and fruits are several locally made food items worth seeking out. Homeboy Bakery, an LA-based do-good social enterprise organization, sells fresh-baked breads, pastries, and specialty goods; Coldwater

Canyon Provisions brings its jams, jellies, marmalades, and pickles; and Mama Musubi's portable Japanese rice balls make for great snacking while shopping.

Tashkent Produce
5340 Laurel Canyon Boulevard, Valley Village
Opened nearly two decades ago, this eastern European market boasts an incredible take-out stall for Uzbek cooking. Walk toward the back of the store to find several kinds of borscht, a splendid selection of cold appetizers, like pâté, cheese, mushrooms, and eggplant, and the national dish of Uzbekistan: plov (rice pilaf with lamb). Pastries and cakes, as well as imported German breads, round out the market's impressive selection.

Valley Relics Museum
7900 Balboa Boulevard, Van Nuys
Housed in two airplane hangars at the Van Nuys Airport, the Valley Relics Museum has an incredible collection of memorabilia celebrating the Valley's contributions to greater Los Angeles's aerospace, film, and culinary industries. The museum is a must-see for those fascinated by Los Angeles restaurant history; the collection of neon signs and menus from bygone restaurants is particularly noteworthy. Don't leave without snagging a Pioneer Chicken T-shirt from the gift shop.

Compton
Crenshaw
El Segundo
Gardena
Harbor City
Hawthorne
Hermosa
  Beach
Inglewood

Jefferson Park
Long Beach
Manhattan
  Beach
Redondo Beach
Torrance
Watts
West Adams
Windsor Hills

SOUT

THE SOU

6

H LA &
UTH BAY

SOUTH LA &
THE SOUTH BAY

DINING

1. Ali'i Fish Company
2. The Arthur J
3. Banadir Somali Restaurant
4. Coni'Seafood
5. Dulan's Soul Food Kitchen
6. Earle's on Crenshaw
7. Gardena Bowl Coffee Shop
8. Harold & Belle's
9. Hawkins House of Burgers
10. Highly Likely
11. Hilltop Coffee + Kitchen, Inglewood
12. Holbox
13. Ichimiann
14. Izakaya Hachi
15. Jerusalem Chicken
16. Koshiji
17. Love & Salt
18. Mizlala West Adams
19. Mr. Fries Man
20. Otafuku
21. Phanny's
22. Roscoe's House of Chicken N Waffles
23. The Serving Spoon
24. Sunday Gravy
25. Sushi Chitose
26. Tamaen Japanese BBQ
27. The Wood
28. Zam Zam Foods

SHOPPING

1. Boccato's Groceries
2. Continental Gourmet Market
3. Giuliano's Delicatessen
4. La Española Meats
5. Lee Heng Market
6. Mitsuwa Marketplace

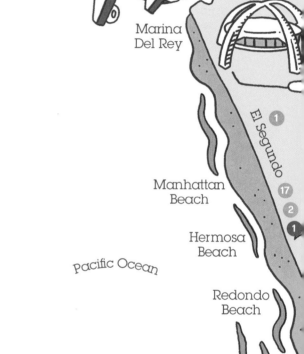

Mar Vista

Marina Del Rey

El Segundo

Manhattan Beach

Hermosa Beach

Pacific Ocean

Redondo Beach

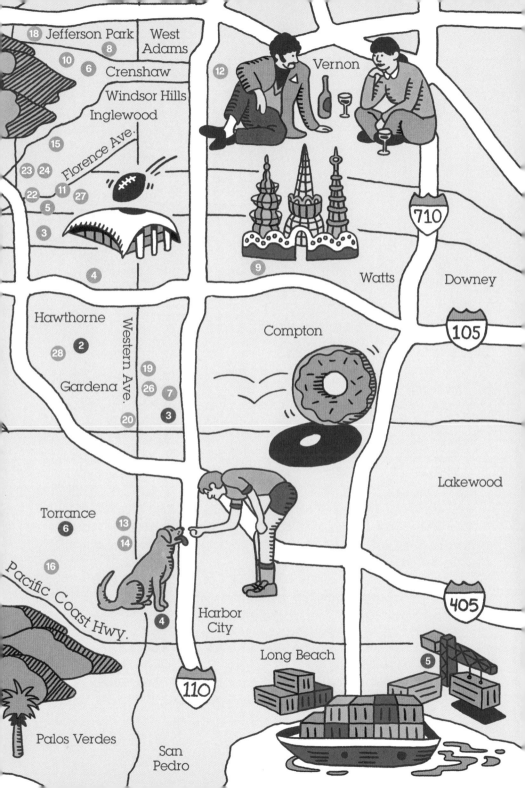

SOUTH LA & THE SOUTH BAY
DINING

South LA covers a wide swath of Southern California. The massive area—it's more than 51 square miles—is filled with a collection of smaller cities and independent neighborhoods that represent an important cultural cross section of Los Angeles. The historic area known as Inglewood, with its vibrant Latinx and Black communities, is home to soulful mom-and-pop joints and has in recent years seen a swath of restaurant openings, thanks to new development in the area like the seventy-thousand-seat entertainment and sports complex SoFi Stadium. (The Kia Forum, still a fan favorite for concerts, is in Inglewood, too.) To the east, Watts, Compton, and Lynwood (and to the south, the city of Hawthorne) are known for old-school classics, while the West Adams neighborhood has seen an influx of developers infiltrating the area. That has translated to both an invigorated restaurant scene and concerns about gentrification.

Meanwhile, the part of town south of LAX and north of Long Beach—which encompasses the bougie seaside enclave of Manhattan Beach, more laid-back Hermosa Beach and Redondo Beach, and the city of Torrance, with its high concentration of Korean and Japanese Americans—feels like its own section of Los Angeles County, complete with a beachy vibe and cultural diversity apparent in its many neighborhoods. Formerly home to three Japanese car companies, the area still hosts a bevy of excellent Japanese restaurants, though Korean, Brazilian, Hawaiian, and even Oaxacan fare are now highlights, too.

1. Ali'i Fish Company

409 East Grand Avenue, El Segundo

Few of this Hawaiian restaurant's competitors, of which there are several just south of LAX in El Segundo, can claim they source their fish straight from the Honolulu fish auction. On top of that, the team behind Ali'i Fish Company dishes up an impressive ahi burger, nostalgic fish nuggets, and ultra-fresh poke—all great options to enjoy on the restaurant's shaded patio.

2. The Arthur J

903 Manhattan Avenue, Manhattan Beach

Chef David LeFevre is essentially the chef-kingpin of Manhattan Beach, with several wildly popular restaurants. His newest venture, the Arthur J, is a fancy steak house that sports some serious retro vibes. The steaks rank among the best in Los Angeles. Exceptional sides and a diverse wine list round out this ocean-side restaurant that is sure to withstand the test of time, with its mid-century-modern feel and charming old-school service.

3. Banadir Somali Restaurant

137 Arbor Vitae Street, Inglewood

Banadir Somali Restaurant, an unfussy order-at-the-counter spot in Inglewood, is among the only Somali restaurants in Los Angeles. All of the halal meats are marinated, then slow-roasted for three hours and served with a simple salad and sides of rice and bas bas (a traditional bright green sauce made with basil, jalapeno, and cilantro, shown opposite), which packs a heated punch.

4. Coni'Seafood

3544 West Imperial Highway, Inglewood

One of LA's best Mexican seafood restaurants is also an Inglewood classic. Coni'Seafood continues to wow weary LAX travelers and locals alike. The marlin tacos alone are worth the trip, but it's the big platter of pescado zarandeado, a whole grilled snook (page 101) served with house-made tortillas, that really turns heads.

5. Dulan's Soul Food Kitchen

202 East Manchester Boulevard, Inglewood

A bona fide Los Angeles institution, twenty-plus-year-old Dulan's has a location in Inglewood as well as one in Crenshaw.

If they're not sold out, opt for the famous gravy-laden stewed oxtails, but any of the heaping platters of fried chicken, smothered chicken, baked fish, and the like, each served with two classic sides and two cornbread muffins, will do the trick. There's also sweet potato pie, and cold sweet tea to wash it all down.

6. Earle's on Crenshaw

3864 Crenshaw Boulevard, Crenshaw

Earle's, a South LA institution found on Crenshaw Boulevard, is run by brothers Cary and Duane Earle. What started in the eighties as a hot dog cart is now a full-service restaurant with a rapid ordering process and a menu that includes vegan dogs, excessively decadent chili dogs, burgers, and so much more.

7. Gardena Bowl Coffee Shop

15707 South Vermont Avenue, Gardena

This long-standing Gardena classic, a diner located in, yes, a bowling alley, has been a neighborhood destination for breakfast served all day and Hawaiian-style dishes like the comforting noodle soup wonton saimin and a fried rice plate served with Portuguese sausage, roast pork, green onions, eggs, and teriyaki sauce.

BEYOND RESTAURANTS

Coffee Shops:
The Boy & The Bear
Hi-Fi Espresso
Sip & Sonder
South LA Cafe

Bars:
1010 Wine & Events
The Bar at Johnny's
Cork & Batter
Mandrake

Bakeries:
Colossus
Little French Bakery
Sweet Red Peach
Sweet Wheat

Ice Cream:
Bruster's Real Ice Cream
Jamz Creamery
Kansha Creamery
Scoops

8. Harold & Belle's

2920 West Jefferson Boulevard, Jefferson Park

After more than fifty years, Jefferson Park mainstay Harold & Belle's still rocks a menu of Louisiana favorites for a large and loyal local clientele. Come for Creole-style favorites like fried oysters, gumbo, jambalaya, and shrimp-and-crawfish étouffée. Now run by third-generation family owners, the restaurant even offers vegan options for the plant-based crowd.

9. Hawkins House of Burgers

11603 Slater Street, Watts

Endless fans flock to Hawkins in Watts, beguiled by the towering burgers that come fresh off the grill. The Colossal Burger, for instance, comes loaded with pastrami, while the Leaning Tower of Watts is a meaty wonder containing three patties, pastrami, a hot link, eggs, chili, and bacon. The space across from Nickerson Gardens (the largest public housing development west of the Mississippi) carries plenty of charm.

10. Highly Likely

4310 West Jefferson Boulevard, West Adams

A perfect all-day café to spend an afternoon at, this West Adams favorite is bright, beautiful, and cheery, with great music to accompany chef Kat Turner's thoughtful, leveled-up breakfast burritos, salads, black-rice bowls, and sandwiches. For example, the Li'l Chicky sandwich—tempura-fried chicken, zesty labneh, minty slaw, Kewpie mayo, and pickled onions on milk bread—is a notch above your basic sando.

11. Hilltop Coffee + Kitchen, Inglewood

170 North La Brea Avenue, Inglewood

Daytime fare (breakfast sandwiches, open-faced "Hilltop Droptops" toasts, waffles) and good coffee are always in order at Hilltop Coffee + Kitchen. But this location has something most cafés don't: a cozy, spacious interior that's in central Inglewood. There's a similar wide-open layout and menu at the View Park–Windsor Hills location.

12. Holbox

3655 South Grand Avenue, South LA

Seafood-centric, James Beard–nominated Holbox, a teensy counter restaurant located within the South LA food hall Mercado La Paloma, spotlights sparklingly fresh local ingredients from Southern California and Baja California in artfully plated coastal Mexican preparations. Menu highlights include ceviches, cocteles, and tostadas, along with simpler preparations of Yucatánean and Baja specialties, including blood clams.

13. Ichimiann
1618 Cravens Avenue, Torrance

Ichimiann, a humble soba and udon factory, is a wonderful place for a casual lunch in Old Torrance. The zaru soba (chilled noodles with soy dipping sauce) is the main draw, but a lot of the soupy cold or hot noodle bowls are excellent, too. The texture of the noodles is unbeatable, with a firm bite and gentle buckwheat flavor. Note it's cash only.

14. Izakaya Hachi
1880 West Carson Street, Torrance

Torrance is home to a bevy of izakayas and drink-friendly Japanese restaurants. Hachi, located in a strip mall, has an impressive menu of after-work Japanese drinking dishes, from pressed saba sushi to grilled chicken skewers. Get together a group and fill your mahogany table with pitchers of Asahi and platters of pork toro and beef tongue.

15. Jerusalem Chicken
4448 West Slauson Avenue, Windsor Hills

If a delightful punch in the taste buds is needed, get to fast-casual Jerusalem

Chicken in Windsor Hills and order the lemon garlic chicken. Be warned, it is full-flavored—savory, pungent, and so incredibly juicy. The bed of rice absorbs plenty of the sauce as well. This restaurant also boasts some of the city's best hummus.

16. Koshiji
22807 Hawthorne Boulevard, Torrance

Yakitori is one of the best forays into Japanese drinking food, and this tiny strip-mall spot in Torrance checks many of the boxes, with high-quality chicken and other meats grilled over binchotan charcoal. Order up some beer, pick up a bunch of skewers, and enjoy a festive meal the Japanese way.

17. Love & Salt
317 Manhattan Beach Boulevard, Manhattan Beach

Now an established Manhattan Beach classic, Love & Salt serves California-Italian fare from restaurateur Sylvie Gabriele. Beach town locals flock here for the reliable, well-executed menu of pastas, pizzas, salads, and entrees in a bustling modern ambience along Manhattan Beach Boulevard's main restaurant drag.

18. Mizlala West Adams
5400 West Adams Boulevard, West Adams

A seat on the cozy shaded patio outfitted with mismatched chairs is the ideal spot to try Mizlala's shawarma, lamb or beef kafta, and fish kebabs—all considered some of the best Middle Eastern food in Los Angeles. When you're ready to cool off, head inside to the order counter and treat yourself to a halva cinnamon or salted caramel tahini shake.

19. Mr. Fries Man
14800 South Western Avenue, Gardena

Craig and Dorothy Batiste started putting incredible, colorful ingredients on French fries in 2016, first serving out of their home kitchen and now expanded to multiple locations across Los Angeles (and even into Las Vegas). In less than a year, they've sold more than twenty franchises, but it all started with the cheery yellow-roofed original in Gardena. Try the Beyond Meat–loaded fries for a plant-based tray of comfort.

20. Otafuku
16525 South Western Avenue, Gardena

One of Gardena's long-time izakayas, this virtually hidden restaurant is hugely popular with the after-work crowd, though it's also a fantastic place to try home-style Japanese dishes and handmade noodles. And celebrity chef David Chang raves about the eel tempura here, so it's worth a try if it's on the menu.

21. Phanny's
1021 South Pacific Coast Highway, Redondo Beach
Redondo Beach's enduring breakfast burrito specialist has a great coffee menu and fantastic burritos that should provide enough caloric intake for long days at the beach. It's been turning out tortillas stuffed with everything from bacon to carne asada since 1982.

22. Roscoe's House of Chicken N Waffles
621 West Manchester Boulevard, Inglewood
Get the classic waffles and fried chicken combination at this LA icon, a diner-style soul-food institution and now mini chain that originally opened in Hollywood in 1975 and has attracted everyone from Stevie Wonder to President Barack Obama. Wash down your order with the signature Eclipse, made with orange juice, fruit punch, and lemonade.

23. The Serving Spoon
1403 Centinela Avenue, Inglewood
This family-owned Inglewood diner has served breakfasts and lunches with a side of friendly service,

making it a neighborhood mainstay, since 1982. You're there for the generous combo plates of soul food; must-orders include cheese grits with catfish and eggs, collard greens, candied yams, or chicken and waffles.

24. Sunday Gravy
1122 Centinela Avenue, Inglewood
This brother-and-sister-owned restaurant offers straightforward Italian American fare in Inglewood. Look for red checkered tablecloths, affordable glasses of wine, and the genre's greatest hits, like cheesy garlic bread, lasagna, and house-made fettuccine with alfredo sauce.

25. Sushi Chitose
402 South Pacific Coast Highway Redondo Beach
Perhaps no one does affordable sushi (a hallmark of South Bay dining) in the area better than Sushi Chitose. The omakase at this cheery little standalone spot on the Pacific Coast Highway in Redondo Beach starts at $75 and might be one of the best bang-for-your-buck sushi experiences in the city.

26. Tamaen Japanese BBQ
Tozai Plaza, 15476 South Western Avenue, Gardena
The Japanese tabletop grilled meat at this minimalist Gardena restaurant is marked by a devotion to truly amazing quality, like dry-aged or even Wagyu

QR CODES
for our online
guides to these
neighborhoods:

INGLEWOOD

SOUTH BAY

SOUTH LA

cuts, served in a fantastic steplike cutting board on the table. Sides are great, too, with kimchi and other banchan that aren't quite as aggressively spiced as one might find in Koreatown. Seeing as the focus here is on high-end meats, the prices can be sky-high.

27. The Wood
129 North Market Street, Inglewood

The Wood is part sports bar, part weekend lounge, and part daytime hot spot for classic barbecue fare like brisket, links, and pulled pork. This do-it-all Inglewood destination is a prime stop into and out of LAX, or before events at SoFi Stadium.

28. Zam Zam Foods
13645/49 South Inglewood Avenue, Hawthorne

The stripped-down Zam Zam Market, with its fluorescent lighting and sparsely stocked grocery shelves, continues to be one of the best places for Pakistani food in LA, with a regularly changing menu cooked by a husband-and-wife team that focuses on flavor over anything else. Call ahead to see what's being served that day, because the offerings might range from chicken biryani to beef kebabs, and be sure to get plenty of naan, too.

SOUTH LA & THE SOUTH BAY
SHOPPING

Specialty food stores abound within the southern portion of Los Angeles. Whether you are preparing for a day at the beach, a sunset picnic, or just looking to stock some local specialties in the vacation rental, the variety and quality of edible options is nothing short of impressive. Best of all, the featured shops tend to carry packaged foodstuffs that make it possible to bring a taste of LA home.

1. Boccato's Groceries

3127 Manhattan Avenue, Hermosa Beach

Consider this quintessential Italian deli and grocery store a must-stop for curating beach day provisions. In addition to a robust sandwich menu that includes cold-cut classics with salami, turkey, and ham, you'll also find hot sandwiches piled high with carnitas and pastrami. Sergio Boccato, who owns Larchmont Village Wine and Cheese, also runs this shop.

2. Continental Gourmet Market

12921 Prairie Avenue, Hawthorne

Opened in 1980, the charming Continental Gourmet Market offers a myriad of Latin American prepared and packaged foods. The house-special Argentine empanadas, flaky-golden parcels stuffed with spicy beef, chicken, ham and cheese, and more, are a highlight. The impressive butcher counter offers Argentine meat of all stripes (parrillada, chorizo sausage, blood sausage) for home grilling.

3. Giuliano's Delicatessen

1138 W Gardena Boulevard, Gardena

Step into Giuliano's Delicatessen for a serious time warp with an Italian American bent. Opened in 1952 by Frances and Gaetano Giuliano, the shop takes great pride in its prepared foods, offering spaghetti sauce, cookies, meatballs, and sausages prepared the old-fashioned way. The deli's torpedo sandwich is adored by regulars and newcomers alike.

4. La Española Meats

25020 Doble Avenue, Harbor City

Come for the stellar selection of imported Spanish groceries and stay for the Saturdays-only paella handmade by Juana and Frank Faraone since 1982. Juana, who hails from Valencia, prepares her saffron-kissed bomba rice with chicken, seafood, beans, peppers, and three kinds of sausages.

5. Lee Heng Market

2211 E Anaheim Street, Long Beach

This small Cambodian market is renowned throughout the Southern California Khmer community for its scratch-made sausages. Sold frozen and in packs large and small, the pork sausages brimming with aromatics are labeled red for spicy and green for classic. Also on hand to round out one's Cambodian pantry are various pickles, fresh papaya, and dipping sauces.

6. Mitsuwa Marketplace

3525 West Carson Street, Torrance

Japanese food lovers would do well prioritizing a visit to the Mitsuwa Marketplace at Del Amo Fashion Center in Torrance. Peruse the fully stocked shelves for goods imported straight from Japan—the selection of cookies (Pocky) and candies (KitKat) always make for crowd-pleasing souvenirs. Don't shop on an empty stomach—swing into the impressive food court for Hokkaido-style ramen at Santouka, mochi doughnuts at Mochill, and curry rice bowls at Sutadon-ya.

BEST SUSHI, TACOS, AND BURGERS

By Hillary Dixler Canavan and Lesley Suter

DESPERATELY SEEKING SUSHI

Sushi restaurants have been a staple of Los Angeles dining since the 1960s (the first sushi restaurants actually opened as early as 1904). In the decades to follow, LA's appetite for sushi—particularly high-end omakase service—helped launch sushi into the American mainstream. Today, Los Angeles is spoiled for choice; here are some of the best.

The Brothers Sushi
21418 Ventura Boulevard, Woodland Hills
Veteran sushi chef Mark Okuda combines classic dry-aged fish and creative presentations in an elegant space in the Valley.

Hama Sushi
213 Windward Avenue, Venice
Head to this Little Tokyo institution for a rollicking crowd and excellent no-frills sushi. As the sign says: NO TEMPURA, NO TERIYAKI. NO NOODLE, NO RICE ALONE.

Hamasaku
11043 Santa Monica Boulevard, Sawtelle
Skip the saucy rolls and spring for the omakase (page 113), which, at under $125 per person, is among the best value propositions in the city's entire sushi scene.

Kogane
1129 South Fremont Avenue C, Alhambra
While Alhambra is best known for its Chinese cuisine, chefs Fumio Azumi and Kwan-san have made a home (page 12) for their high-end, destination-worthy omakase menu (pro tip: the weekday lunch omakase clocks in at about half the price of the full dinner experience).

Morihiro
3133 Glendale Boulevard, Atwater Village
Sushi legend Morihiro Onodera helms a dream of a restaurant, where he mills his own rice, serves delicate cooked and raw courses on ceramics he made himself, and, naturally, boasts an impressive reservation wait list.

Nozawa Bar

212 North Canon Drive, Beverly Hills

This sushi counter (page 115) is hidden in a small private dining room the back of the Sugarfish in Beverly Hills, but the menu is way more luxe, with bite after bite of meticulously crafted nigiri.

Q

521 West 7th Street, Downtown

The move at this Downtown den, a longtime contender for the top honors in LA sushi rankings, is to book for lunch tasting, which at $150 is half the cost of a dinner omakase.

Shin Sushi

16573 Ventura Boulevard, Encino

The Encino strip-mall setting only adds to the allure of this impressive omakase spot, where chef Taketoshi Azumi presents course after course with a showman's flair.

Shunji Japanese Cuisine

3003 Ocean Park Boulevard, Santa Monica

Shunji has been synonymous with high-end sushi in LA for years. Nabbing a seat in front of chef Shunji Nakao, or with his partner, chef Miki Takahiro, at the other counter, is a must for any sushi lover.

Sushi Gen

422 East 2nd Street, Little Tokyo

Head to this Little Tokyo icon (page 102) for an amazingly priced sashimi lunch special or level up with dinner at the bar.

Sushi Kisen

1108 South Baldwin Avenue B6, Arcadia

A tremendous value at lunch and a guide-your-own adventure at dinner, this SGV charmer is perfect for anyone who wants to keep an eye on cost without sacrificing fine technique.

Sushi Note

13447 Ventura Boulevard, Sherman Oaks

You're headed to this essential Valley restaurant for its wine as much as its stunning nigiri. You can add a $75 wine pairing to go with an omakase dinner, or go by the glass or bottle; likewise, along with an $140 omakase, you can order sushi a la carte.

Sushi Takeda

123 Astronaut Ellison South Onizuka Street Little Toyko

From splurge-y to-go lunches to twenty-plus-course omakase dinners, chef Hide Takeda has a menu for every mood at his Little Tokyo stunner.

TACO CITY

Tacos are the signature food of the city, and you'll find versions representing every Mexican region under the sun, as well as wild manifestations of the city's cultural mishmash all tucked into tortillas. From trucks to sit-down spots, here's what not to miss.

Burritos La Palma
5120 Peck Road, El Monte

Burritos are, in fact, a type of taco, and this family-owned company (page 35) specializes in petite, Northern Mexican–style burritos, filled with juicy beef birria on a fresh flour tortilla.

El Ruso
1647 West Sunset Boulevard, Echo Park

At this roving Eastside truck, find Sonora-influenced carne asada (grilled meat) tacos in stretchy flour tortillas, and massive Sonoran sobaqueras (burritos wrapped in enormous tortillas) filled with rich chile colorado.

Gish Bac
4163 West Washington Boulevard, Mid-City

Oaxacan barbacoa made from slow pit-roasted lamb fills the tortillas at this cash-only midcity legend.

Guisados
Multiple locations

Founded in Boyle Heights, this local mini chain focuses on what it sounds like: guisados, or braised stews, on house-made corn tortillas.

La Flor de Yucatán
1800 Hoover Street, MacArthur Park

Order a Yucatan-style taco de relleno negro, where shredded turkey cooked in a black achiote paste is contrasted by pickled red onions and creamy guacamole, from this spot near MacArthur Park.

Leo's Tacos
Multiple locations

A fleet of trucks are behind crimson mounds of al pastor, or sweet marinated pork, trimmed from vertical spits finished with the spectacle of flying chunks of pineapple.

Los Originales Tacos Arabes de Puebla
3600 East Olympic Boulevard, Boyle Heights

The Villegas family brings in traditional products from Puebla—including the special tortillas, called pan árabe—and prepares their tacos with tender pork and a tangy chipotle salsa.

Mariscos Jalisco
3040 East Olympic Boulevard, Boyle Heights

Raul Ortega's iconic Boyle Heights mariscos truck (page 37) serves one of the city's finest tacos: tacos dorados de camarones, spiced, golden deep-fried shrimp come garnished with avocado and fresh salsa roja.

Sonoratown
5610 San Vicente Boulevard, Downtown

The calling card here (page 71) is the best-in-class flour tortillas. Try them with the smoky grilled carne asada.

Tacos 1986
609 South Spring Street, Downtown

What began as a roving taco stand has blossomed into a bona fide mini chain and local sensation, known for its Tijuana-style tacos stuffed with carne asada, adobada, and the perron—a flour tortilla filled with pinto beans, carne asada, guacamole, and melted jack cheese. Locations are now throughout the city, from Santa Monica to Burbank to Pasadena. Try them all, or the DTLA original.

Tacos Baja
Multiple locations

One of the original fish taco stands in Southern California, opened in 1998 by cofounders Lourdes Toscano and Martin Vásquez, features a highly guarded, secret tempura batter for Ensenada-style fried fish and shrimp tacos.

Tacos Don Cuco
752 South Fetterly Avenue, East Los Angeles

This father-and-son team excels at tacos, mulitas (a cross between a taco and a quesadilla), and tostadas topped with chopped chicken and pork shoulder steaks. They all come dressed with diced onions and cilantro, mild tomato salsa, and a heaping spoonful of creamy guacamole.

Tacos La Güera
Multiple locations

This truck is as beloved for its al pastor as for its suadero, or brisket, tacos, but the real ones come for the offal like chorizo, hog's maw, and chitterlings.

Tamales Elenas y Antojito
Wilmington Avenue & East 110th Street, Watts

The guisados, or stews, are perfect for making your own tacos, but try the tacos dorados, or crunchy shell tacos, too, with varieties like pescadillas (crispy fish tacos) and spicy beef barbacoa. The former Bell Gardens restaurant is now a truck, which parks at Wilmington Avenue and 109th Street in Watts. The menu is smaller but the impact is just as large.

Teddy's Red Tacos
Multiple locations

Fluorescent red beef birria (page 59) tacos served with a cup of slow-simmered consommé are the draw at this local mini chain of stands and trucks throughout the city.

BURGERTOWN, USA

Burgers are one of the quintessential foods of Southern California, in no small part due to the role of drive-thru and drive-up dining in the area. With every style from smash burgers to thick pub burgers, Los Angeles is a burger lover's paradise.

Amboy Quality Meats & Delicious Burgers
727 North Broadway, Chinatown

For a simple take on a classic cheeseburger, order the Fancy DH Burger, a glistening ten-ounce dry-aged patty topped with provolone cheese, caramelized onions, pickles, and garlic confit mayo on a toasted sesame brioche bun.

The Apple Pan
10801 West Pico Boulevard, West LA

You've sidled up to the Apple Pan's old-fashioned diner-style counter (page 113) for a Hickory Burger: A house hickory sauce, mayonnaise, and pickles come standard, but do consider taking the add-on option of Tillamook cheddar.

Burgerlords
Multiple locations

The gold standard for meat-free burgers in LA, the Burgerlords burger comes from a fierce, delicious commitment to keeping the "veggie" in "veggie burger."

Goldburger
5623 York Boulevard, Highland Park

A photo-worthy smashburger with crispy edges but enough heft to still have some bite awaits at this Highland Park favorite (page 36; or you can head to the Los Feliz location if that's closer).

Hawkins House of Burgers
11603 Slater Street, Watts

The classic burgers are great, but the pastrami-topped monsters are what you're here for (page 128).

HiHo Cheeseburger
Multiple locations

The namesake burger here is an impressive double-decker with two New Zealand Wagyu beef patties, cheese, ketchup, onion jam, lettuce, mustard, and pickles.

Hinano Cafe
15 Washington Boulevard, Venice

Cooks griddle burger patties right behind the bar at this Venice favorite (page 148).

Irv's Burgers
1000 South La Brea Avenue, West Hollywood

This legendary Route 66 burger stand (page 90) doesn't skimp on toppings: The Big Irv comes with pastrami, a hot dog, and more on top.

Yellow Paper Burger
Monterey Park
(address given upon payment via Instagram)

Clad in red jumpsuits, the Yellow Paper Burger crew pops up at sceney Eastside spots like Altadena Beverage and Club Tee Gee to sling double-stacked burgers with plenty of cheese and shredded lettuce.

Moo's Craft Barbecue
2118 North Broadway, Cypress Park

Peppery, smoky, and thick-cut, this cheeseburger makes a compelling case for heading to a barbecue joint for your next great burger.

The Oinkster
2005 Colorado Boulevard, Eagle Rock

Way over on the Eastside in Eagle Rock, you'll find the must-order Royale, piled high with pastrami, chili, bacon, and cheese—a nod to the decadence of LA's burger culture.

Original Tommy's World Famous Hamburgers
Mutiple locations

A staple since the 1940s, Tommy's is a taste of chili-topped LA burger history.

Pie 'n Burger
913 East California Boulevard, Pasadena

Perhaps the single most famous restaurant in Pasadena (page 14), old school diner Pie 'n Burger's namesake is covered thick-cut, stacked with tomato, onion, pickles, lettuce, and slathered in special sauce.

Petit Trois
718 North Highland Avenue, Hollywood

There are restaurant burgers, and there is chef Ludo Lefebvre's iconic Big Mec, a double cheeseburger drenched in Bordelaise and served with frites.

The Win-Dow
Multiple locations

An offshoot of Venice's American Beauty restaurant (page 145), the Win-Dow sells affordable, cheesy smash burgers from, yes, windows on Venice's Rose Avenue, on the Venice Beach boardwalk, and in Silver Lake.

Culver City
Mar Vista
Santa Monica
Venice

WEST

7

TSIDE

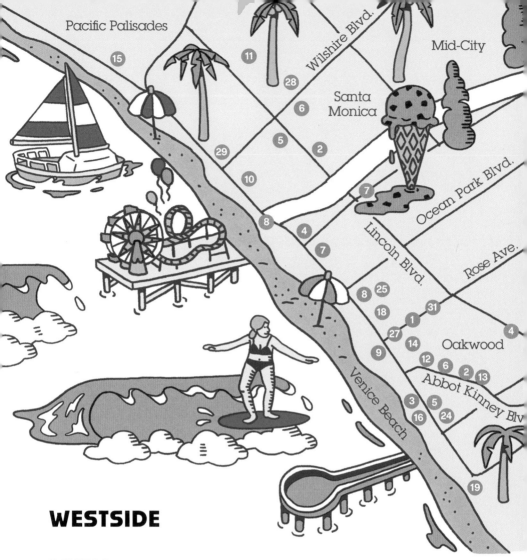

WESTSIDE

DINING

1. American Beauty
2. Bay Cities Italian Deli & Bakery
3. Belles Beach House
4. Capo
5. Cassia
6. Citrin
7. Cobi's

8. Crudo e Nudo
9. Dudley Market
10. Elephante
11. Father's Office
12. Felix
13. Gjelina
14. Gjusta
15. The Golden Bull

16. Gran Blanco
17. Hatchet Hall
18. Heavy Handed
19. Hinano Cafe
20. Honey's Kettle
21. Lodge Bread Company
22. Mayura Indian Restaurant
23. Night + Market Sahm

WESTSIDE
DINING

So much of the aspirational Los Angeles way of life is being minutes from its wide, sandy beaches—and there's no better way to do so than spending time in Santa Monica and Venice. Santa Monica has its iconic amusement-park-topped pier and outdoor shopping destination the Third Street Promenade. It also offers just about every type of restaurant (including many tourist traps that can be skipped). You'll find everything from incredible sandwiches for a beach picnic to restaurants with enchanting ocean views to high-end French bistro food for a date night just steps from the water.

Nearby, Venice has undergone some dramatic changes, shifting from an artists' community to arguably the coolest neighborhood in all of Los Angeles. The beach itself still has a gritty, counterculture feel to it, but it's not a cheap place to live or dine, thanks in part to Abbot Kinney's emergence as a cool-kid shopping and dining street. It's a fantastic place to spend a day (this is a good place to hang out before your flight to avoid traffic jams). People-watch at Gjusta, explore the restaurants on popular Rose Avenue, or have some of the best handmade pasta in the city.

Finally, some of the city's most exciting openings are happening in the shopping and entertainment hub of Culver City, which is home to studios (and now big tech companies), a strollable downtown, and iconic fried-chicken spot Honey's Kettle. Sit down for a meal or grab it on your way to the airport, where you'll be the envy of the entire boarding area.

3. Belles Beach House
24 Windward Avenue,
Venice

The beach seems to come right to diners and drinkers at Belles Beach House, the Tulum-meets-tiki stunner just steps off the Venice boardwalk, where the coolest of the Westside set hang out. Part bar, part restaurant, this is the place to smell the salty ocean and maybe see someone famous as you sip a mai tai and dine on pan-Asian dishes with Polynesian influences like huli huli chicken.

1. American Beauty
425 Rose Avenue,
Venice

Under twinkling lights over a massive courtyard, Westsiders enjoy updated steakhouse classics courtesy of chef Elisha Ben-Haim at this mostly open-air restaurant on Venice's bustling Rose Avenue. Simplicity is the name of the game here: Think thick steaks grilled over almond wood and finished with butter and salt, grilled flatbread served with smoked honey and labneh, and must-order hash browns stuffed with melted onion and sour cream. With a casual vibe, two-hundred-plus wines on offer, and excellent cocktails, American Beauty is the type of restaurant that makes a big night out feel fun, not fussy.

2. Bay Cities Italian Deli & Bakery
1517 Lincoln Boulevard,
Santa Monica

This Santa Monica Italian deli/bakery has been serving the Westside crowd since opening in 1925 and is the spot to grab a sandwich if you're hitting the beach, offering what is likely the most iconic sandwich in all of Los Angeles: the Godmother. Bay Cities' signature sub is filled with prosciutto, ham, capicola, mortadella, Genoa salami, and provolone cheese, all contained in a crusty Italian-style filone roll. During the lunchtime rush, order ahead online or grab a number at the entrance and pass the time waiting for your turn by browsing their well-stocked aisles of Italian, Greek, French, and Middle Eastern delicacies.

4. Capo
1810 Ocean Avenue,
Santa Monica

This staple on Santa Monica's Ocean Avenue continues to delight a never-ending stream of Westside customers with fine wines, robust pastas, and wood-grilled meats in a serene dining room with an exposed-beam ceiling. The restaurant's staying power is a testament to owner Bruce Marder, a longtime LA restaurateur.

5. Cassia
1314 7th Street,
Santa Monica

Bryant and Kim Luu-Ng's Cassia, heralded by critics and diners alike for its elevated French-Vietnamese fare, is housed in Santa Monica's historic Telephone Building, an Art Deco landmark. Some of Cassia's greatest hits include the kaya toast, beef rendang, laksa, and chickpea curry. Excellent cocktails, a gorgeous dining room, and an expansive patio all add to the restaurant's appeal as a true crowd-pleaser.

6. Citrin

1104 Wilshire Boulevard, Santa Monica

Renowned Westside chef Josiah Citrin's namesake Michelin-starred restaurant inside the former Mélisse offers a four-course French-California tasting menu, though à la carte options are available, too. Two-Michelin-star Mélisse, which now occupies its own space in the building, offers an even more high-end gastronomical experience.

7. Cobi's

2104 Main Street, Santa Monica

Main Street Santa Monica was a somewhat sleepy stretch of shops and restaurants just blocks off the Pacific, until an abundance of openings over the past few years gave it a much-needed shot in the arm. One of the early newcomers was Cobi's, a Southeast Asian–inspired dinner spot that has all the charm of a grandma's home (or leafy backyard), along with well-made curries, raw fish preparations, butter chicken, tartare, and grilled branzino that will please a crowd. Ask the

servers for a solid bottle of natural wine to pair with the meal, and don't sleep on the excellent brunch menu.

8. Crudo e Nudo

2724 Main Street, Santa Monica

Another major player in the recent Main Street Santa Monica dining renaissance? Crudo e Nudo, which strives for simplicity and pristine seafood in its diminutive sidewalk layout. The raw-fish specialist serves fresh oysters, Italian-style crudo, and juicy natural wines to match, all served with care but without pretense. Order a bunch of seafaring treats at the counter, then take a seat in the parklet and watch the world go by. Or try Isla, their second venture just down the street, for wood-fired skewers.

9. Dudley Market

9 Dudley Avenue, Venice

This jewel box of a restaurant serves impeccably fresh seafood mere steps away from the sand on Venice Beach. Slide into a cozy table and order a variety of oysters, crudo, sashimi, shrimp quesadillas, and a great burger (a Wagyu patty topped with dill aioli, fresh arugula, and a bacon-caramelized onion cheddar jam), then choose a glass or a bottle from one of the Westside's most vibrant selections of natural wine.

10. Elephante

1332 2nd Street, Santa Monica

Visitors to Santa Monica invariably look for a stylish, easygoing restaurant with a terrific view, and most of the places in this category veer too pricey or unimpressive food-wise. This isn't the case with Elephante, which boasts clean views of the Pacific Ocean from its rooftop location, but also serves tasty salads, wood-fired pizzas, and fresh pastas that are a cut above tourist traps. With its breezy, lounge-y vibes, it's also an ideal spot to grab a cocktail and watch the sunset.

11. Father's Office

1018 Montana Avenue, Santa Monica

Sang Yoon was an early proponent of the gourmet burger, when he decided to offer one at his Santa Monica gastropub in 2000 (page 104). Going beyond that burger—topped with its now-famous and never-modified combination of bacon, arugula, Gruyère, blue cheese, caramelized onions—everything from the duck salad to steak frites and even mushrooms go fantastically with the extensive list of craft beers on deck. Just don't ask for ketchup, or any changes, actually. Really.

from squash blossoms to house-made chorizo, rotating market-inspired salads, seasonal pastas, and larger-format dishes like slow-cooked short ribs. Because it's always packed, coming for an early lunch is a solid move.

12. Felix

1023 Abbot Kinney Boulevard, Venice

Chef Evan Funke's dedication to serving some of the best pizza and handmade pasta in the city has yielded tremendous results at his chic trattoria on Venice's famed Abbot Kinney Boulevard. The otherworldly handmade pastas are broken down by regions of Italy; you can see it all come to life from the main dining room, which has a view of the restaurant's glass-enclosed "pasta lab." Funke's olive-oil-drenched Sfincione (Sicilian focaccia) and fried squash blossoms are not to be missed.

13. Gjelina

1429 Abbot Kinney Boulevard, Venice

Still as much a cool-kid spot as it was when it opened on Abbot Kinney in 2008, Gjelina serves some of the best vegetables, salads, and pizzas on the Westside (and maybe in the entire city). Loyalists come for heavily blistered pizzas topped with everything

14. Gjusta

320 Sunset Avenue, Venice

There's a reason bakery-and-restaurant Gjusta, the sister to perennial Venice hot spot Gjelina, is always packed: Just about everything that comes out of the massive kitchen—from cured fish plates served with slabs of its folkloric, fresh-baked bread to egg sandwiches to pork posole—is crazy delicious. Grab a number to order at the counter, then enjoy your meal (which should absolutely include a pastry or dessert) at the restaurant's garden seating. And try to come during off-hours to avoid the crowds.

15. The Golden Bull

170 West Channel Road, Santa Monica

Established in 1949, this historic steak house off the Pacific Coast Highway in Santa Monica Canyon reopened in 2018 with a refreshed old-school vibe and fine-tuned chophouse menu. Dinnertime choices cover the classics, including Caesar salad, shrimp cocktail, lamb chops, New York strip, and a bone-in rib eye. Cocktails are equally timeless, with Manhattans and martinis on offer. And while you're there, don't forget to catch a glimpse of the whimsical aquarium behind the bar.

BEYOND RESTAURANTS

Coffee Shops:
10 Speed Coffee
Cognoscenti Coffee
Goodboybob Coffee
    Roasters
Menotti's Coffee Stop

Bars:
The Brig
Chez Jay
Old Man Bar
Roosterfish

Bakeries:
Copenhagen Pastry
Huckleberry Café
Jyan Isaac Bread
Röckenwagner Bakery
    & Café

Ice Cream:
Ginger's Divine Ice
    Creams
Mateo's Ice Cream &
    Fruit Bars
Sweet Rose Creamery

16. Gran Blanco

80 Windward Avenue,
Venice

Gran Blanco is among Venice's best natural wine bars, a sexy, cozy, and dimly lit dinner-and-drinks hangout right under the iconic Venice sign and steps from the beach. Here, hip kids mix with surfers, tourists, and everyone else inside the whitewashed evening space, which also serves tasty snacks like curry fried chicken and buffalo cauliflower and well-made spritzy cocktails. Nearby Great White, from the same team, is a sun-soaked daytime favorite.

17. Hatchet Hall

12517 Washington Boulevard,
Culver City

This sprawling Culver City institution, with its generous wooden bar, ample wallpapered dining room, and a plethora of outdoor seating, is known for its Southern affectation and boundless energy. Yes, there are expected dishes like corn bread and roasted meats on the very long menu, but there is a lightness to the food and a modern California sensibility that marries well with the usual flavors. Try everything from wild blue shrimp slathered in Old Bay butter to a hearth-grilled pork chop with fennel pollen, all served on mismatched vintage plates.

18. Heavy Handed

2912 Main Street,
Santa Monica

Rocking a colorful street-art energy and sprawling mini-parklet-style outdoor dining area, Heavy Handed draws in burger aficionados looking for ground short-rib patties topped with American cheese, crunchy pickles, and special sauce. With crunchy beef tallow fries, a compact list of natural wine and craft beers, and a dessert of swoon-worthy soft serve, it's hard to think of a more satisfying quick meal on Main Street Santa Monica.

19. Hinano Cafe

15 Washington Boulevard,
Venice

Everyone from surfers to aging hippies to finance bros comes to this sixty-plus-year-old Venice Beach institution. That's because one of the city's most beloved dive bars also happens to serve a no-frills burger that's equally beloved (and served with a bag of chips, or Fritos, or Cheetos, no less). The griddled masterpiece can be enjoyed inside while waiting for a turn at one of two pool tables, or at one of the parklet tables while watching the world go by. Just be sure to have cash on hand.

20. Honey's Kettle

9537 Culver Boulevard,
Culver City

This casual Culver City staple makes all of its kettle-fried chicken (shown below) with love—and yes, there's honey around, too. The extra-crisp coating makes for ideal wing eating, leading to happy messes at the table. There's also coleslaw, mashed potatoes, pickles, fresh-baked biscuits, and pies of the pecan, apple, and sweet potato varieties to round out the meal.

21. Lodge Bread Company

11918 Washington Boulevard,
Culver City

With its dedication to an extended fermentation and seasonal whole grains, Lodge Bread Company bakes an exceptional loaf. It's no wonder, then, that bread is the star at this Culver City breakfast and lunch spot: Have it on sandwiches, use it to sop up a flavorful shakshuka, or try it in thick toasted slices topped with ricotta and jam. Lodge also makes a mean sourdough pizza.

22. Mayura Indian Restaurant

10406 Venice Boulevard,
Culver City

Culver City's fantastic Indian restaurant Mayura was a longtime favorite of the late food critic Jonathan Gold, offering an extensive menu with a slew of South Asian favorites, from dosas to lamb korma and daal masala to sweet mango lassi to drink. There's a small selection of beer and wine, too.

23. Night + Market Sahm

2533 Lincoln Boulevard,
Venice

Some of Los Angeles's best Thai food is made with color and care by chef Kris Yenbamroong. This spot doesn't skimp on flavors or heat, making it one of the hottest (in many ways) places to dine in all of Venice (see also page 144).

24. Ospi

2025 Pacific Avenue,
Venice

Located in the former long-time Venice hangout Canal Club's space, rollicking Ospi from *Top Chef* contestant Jackson Kalb and his wife, Melissa Kalb, is making some of the city's best pizzas and pastas. The menu also offers meatballs and larger mains like a crispy branzino, butter chicken (think: chicken parm with vodka sauce), and pork collar. The secret to any order at this clubby spot is a side of the spicy Japanese eggplant and the Frisbee-sized fried provolone with vodka sauce to start.

25. Pasjoli

2732 Main Street,
Santa Monica

Fine-dining vet Dave Beran serves a highly elevated French bistro experience at this gorgeous restaurant outfitted with archways and a marble-top bar. Favorites like the chicken liver–stuffed foie de poulet brioche, steak au poivre, and whole pressed duck continue to please longtime regulars, while the rest of the menu offers California-inspired takes on French fare. One of the most reliable upscale places to eat on the Westside, this Main Street Santa Monica destination has the service and ambience to match the amazing food.

26. Pasta Sisters

3280 Helms Avenue,
Culver City

Chef Paola De Re and her three children opened a plucky little pasta shop in Mid-City in 2015, expanding to a larger restaurant in Culver City a few years later. With approachable pricing and a fast-casual service model, Pasta Sisters draws big lines for polished bowls of spaghetti, tagliatelle, and pappardelle with a customer's choice of sauces that might include pesto, Bolognese, or creamy porcini mushroom. A modern pasta classic, Pasta Sisters has captured the hearts of LA diners.

27. The Rose Venice

220 Rose Avenue,
Venice

Jason Neroni's remake of the iconic 1979 Rose Café is still a neighborhood staple and the type of place that satisfies almost any craving. Need a soy milk latte in the morning? No problem. Thinking grain bowls for lunch? Sure. Want to feast on spaghetti with Santa Barbara uni and sip a great cocktail in the evening? This restaurant megaplex has it all, plus an impressive outdoor patio for people-watching.

28. Rustic Canyon
1119 Wilshire Boulevard,
Santa Monica

One of Santa Monica's most storied and reliable places for modern California cuisine, Rustic Canyon is a showcase of Southern California's seasonal bounty, with dishes like roasted chicken with carrots, walnut, a carrot-top yogurt and molasses, and pecans. Lauded executive chef Jeremy Fox still has a hand in the menu, which changes as new chefs de cuisine put their personal touches on it. But its overall excellence, focus on ingredients, and well-made cocktails remain consistent through the years.

29. Soko
101 Wilshire Boulevard,
Santa Monica

One of Santa Monica's most exciting sushi spots, a tiny eight-seat counter and a smattering of tables set at the side entrance to the Fairmont Miramar hotel are where chef Masa Shimakawa prepares stellar nigiri, sashimi, and other raw Japanese fare. Meaning "storeroom" in Japanese, Soko feels like a hole in the wall, but with the quality of a destination omakase spot. There's everything from a chef's choice omakase to a full à la carte menu in case you want to choose your own sushi adventure.

30. Tito's Tacos
11222 Washington Place,
Culver City

The meat, bean, and cheese burrito is a pro move for those in the know at legendary Tito's in Culver City, even though the hard-shelled tacos topped with shredded cheese earn all the love online and on Instagram. Old-school flavors and the restaurant's signature salsa have combined under the California sunshine into something totally unique since 1959.

31. Wallflower
609 Rose Avenue,
Venice

This longtime spot on Rose Avenue in Venice celebrates the diverse flavors of Indonesia and Southeast Asia. Start with a few street snacks, like the crab rendang dip, before digging into the drunken fried chicken for two or the nasi goreng (Indonesian fried rice, shown below). The signature cocktails here are worth a sip, too.

QR CODES
for our online guides to these neighborhoods:

CULVER CITY

SANTA MONICA

VENICE

WESTSIDE
SHOPPING

With their cooler temps, salt-kissed breezes, and laid-back vibes, there's much to love about Los Angeles's beachside communities. Before heading toward the Pacific, pop into one of these local gems for picnicking essentials. The shopping in this part of town reflects residents' penchant for outdoor living and understated yet stylish aesthetics.

1. Broome Street General Store
8840 Washington Boulevard, Culver City

Founder Sophie Graham stocks this New York–inspired shop with items sourced from across the globe, including gifts for gourmands, like olive oils, spices, and cookbooks. The store donates a percentage of every purchase to organizations dedicated to equality, sustainability, and public education.

2. Burro
1409 Abbot Kinney Boulevard, Venice

A visit to Venice wouldn't be complete without strolling along Abbot Kinney Boulevard, quite possibly the coolest block in America. Stop into Burro for a fun selection of highly giftable items with a California bent. The store's lineup of cookbooks, kitchenware, and other accessories has a way of capturing the West Coast's chill lifestyle just right.

3. ChocoVivo
12469 Washington Boulevard, Mar Vista

Visit this chocolate factory in Mar Vista for a taste of Patricia Tsai's handcrafted bean-to-bar chocolates. Tsai proudly sources all of her cacao from a single grower in Tabasco, Mexico, and processes the beans minimally to preserve its natural flavor profile. The on-site café serves an array of sipping chocolates and even a chocolate chip cookie flight. Available to go are chocolate bars, chocolate butters, hot cocoa mix, and more.

4. General Store

1801 Lincoln Boulevard, Venice

From quirky gifts like a set of morel mushroom beeswax candles to kitchen essentials like a brass pepper mill, Venice's General Store stocks something for every food lover. The selection of ceramic homewares made by local artists is especially of note, including the sturdy serving bowls from Kat and Roger Ceramics and timeless hand-formed stoneware mugs from Mt. Washington Pottery.

5. Gjusta Grocer

105 Windward Avenue, Venice

It can be a pain to snag a reservation at Gjelina (page 147) or to wait in a winding line at Gjusta (page 147), so locals know to swing into Gjusta Grocer instead. The well-stocked Venice market brings together all that's good to eat, from grab-and-go sandwiches to crusty loaves and fresh salads. The house-made condiments, including marinated olive oil, harissa ketchup, and fermented chile hot sauce, make for tremendous edible gifts that offer a taste of Venice at home.

6. Goodies

1219 Abbot Kinney Boulevard, Venice

Goodies manages to strike the perfect balance between style and affordability with its line of minimalist home goods and kitchenware. From ceramic vases to a duo of mugs, every item is priced at $25 or under. Largely made of ceramic, wood, and marble, Goodies' wares can be seamlessly incorporated into any existing color scheme. Goodies has two additional locations in Santa Monica and Atwater Village.

7. Lady & Larder

828 Pico Boulevard, Santa Monica

This itty-bitty shop known for its Instagram-ready cheese and snack platters is the place to go for picnic provisions. The shop's ready-to-go boxes are filled with an array of goodies—from American-produced cheeses to fresh fruit sourced from the Santa Monica, Venice, and Mar Vista farmers' markets and crudites (there's a vegan box, too). To round out any alfresco spread are fresh-baked baguettes sourced from local bakeries, jams, honeys, and more.

8. Santa Monica Farmers Market

Farmers' markets are a year-round ritual throughout the Southland, and the ones held in Santa Monica on Wednesdays and Saturdays from eight A.M. to one P.M. are particularly great. Spanning four city blocks on Arizona Avenue between Second and Fourth Streets, the Santa Monica Farmers Market is a hit with both locals and professional chefs for its impressive selection of locally grown fruits and vegetables. The Wednesday marketplace is the place to be for those who want to rub elbows with LA's finest farm-to-table chefs.

AMAZING PATIOS

Los Angeles has maybe (definitely) the best weather in the country, so outdoor dining is a year-round luxury. Here are some of the prettiest patios and most ravishing rooftops in town.

Bavel
500 Mateo Street, Arts District
Tricked out with potted plants and twinkly lights, the Bavel patio is a dreamy oasis in the industrial Arts District.

Damian
2132 East 7th Place, Arts District
Enrique Olvera's restaurant (page 67) makes the most of its outdoor dining space with sleek lines and uplit trees.

De Buena Planta
2815 Sunset Boulevard, Silver Lake
Feel like you've been transported to Mexico on the lush patio of this Silver Lake stunner (shown above) that serves vegetarian tacos, tostadas, and the like.

Fia
2454 Wilshire Boulevard, Santa Monica
One of the classiest Italian joints in town, also has a beautiful tree-lined patio warmly lit by hanging lights.

Gjusta
320 Sunset Avenue, Venice
The artfully disheveled who's who of Venice gather here for cured fish and baked delights (page 147).

Grandmaster Recorders
1518 North Cahuenga Boulevard, Hollywood
The rooftop at this stylish spot serving modern Italian food boasts sweeping views of the Hollywood Hills.

Hatchet Hall
12517 Washington Boulevard, Culver City
A large yard with picnic tables make for a scenic backdrop to some of the city's favorite Southern fare (page 148).

Michael's
1147 Third Street, Santa Monica
Get your garden party on at this chichi Santa Monica institution (page 102).

Mírame
419 North Canon Drive, Beverly Hills
A seat on the front patio at this gorgeous indoor-outdoor Mexican restaurant is the perfect place to watch Beverly Hills go by.

Mother Tongue
960 North La Brea Avenue, 4th floor, Hollywood
Chef Michael Mina's swank ode to healthy eating has an expansive patio with impressive views.

Salazar
2490 Fletcher Drive, Frogtown
This mostly outdoor taqueria in Frogtown, with its strong margaritas, is an ideal place to spend an afternoon sipping and snacking.

Superba Food + Bread
6530 Sunset Boulevard, Hollywood
The Hollywood location of this all-day café is located in a historic space outfitted with a central tree-lined patio.

FOOD HALLS

LA's food halls are microcosms of the city, housing destination restaurants, diverse mom-and-pops, and buzzy upstarts alongside institutions. When you need a respite from LA's sprawl, here's where to mix and match your meals without the mileage.

Citizen Public Market
9355 Culver Boulevard, Culver City
Grab coffee brewed from house-roasted beans at GoodBoyBob and oysters from Jolly Oyster, and finish with a cocktail at the rooftop Bar Bohemian, a few of the eight vendors at this smaller Culver City food hall.

Far East Plaza
727 North Broadway, Chinatown
Newcomers such as hot-chicken counter Howlin' Rays, burger spot Amboy, and coffee perfectionist Endorffeine have swept in, but some of the standbys like noodle house Kim Chuy and Cantonese restaurant Fortune Gourmet Kitchen anchor this two-story Chinatown mall built in 1979.

Grand Central Market
317 South Broadway, Downtown
If you like food halls, you can't miss LA's grand dame (page 67).

Mercado La Paloma
3655 South Grand Avenue, South LA
This community center founded by a nonprofit is home to the celebrated Yucatecan restaurants Chichen Itza and Holbox (page 128), as well as Taqueria Vista Hermosa's tacos al pastor, Oaxacalifornia's torta oaxaqueña, and Gusina Saraba's Belizean Garifuna dishes.

The Original Farmers Market
6333 West Third Street, Beverly Grove
French at Monsieur Marcel, Cajun at the Gumbo Pot, Korean fried chicken at BHC — there's all that and more at central LA's historic, ever-changing outdoor food hall (page 97) near the Grove.

Row DTLA
777 South Alameda Street, Downtown
The expansive Downtown Row houses the LA outpost of the legendary Pizzeria Bianco (page 70) and its sandwich cousin, Pane Bianco, as well as Taiwanese tasting-menu restaurant Kato (page 68).

The Shops at Santa Anita
400 South Baldwin Avenue, Arcadia
Find some of Asia's best chains all in one place at this San Gabriel Valley mall, including Din Tai Fung (page 12), HaiDiLao Hot Pot, and Marugame Udon.

Steelcraft Long Beach
3768 Long Beach Boulevard, Long Beach
At this outdoor food plaza built out of repurposed shipping containers, assemble lunch with sweet and savory waffles from Waffle Love and tacos from La Taqueria Brand, and wash it all down with one (or a few) of the twenty beers on tap at Smog City Brewing.

Topanga Social
6600 CA-27, Canoga Park
In West Valley, this massive 55,000-square-foot food hall, with multiple bars and hundreds of indoor and outdoor seats, corrals some of LA's hottest food and drink vendors, including Katsu Sando, Tail o' the Pup (page 93), and Mini Kabob.

LA FOOD CALENDAR

There's no shortage of food festivals, events, and pop-ups to check out on any given day in Los Angeles. Sink your teeth into some of these delicious happenings.

Dine LA

Twice a year, restaurants around town participating in Dine LA offer deals on prix fixe lunch and dinner menus intended to encourage diners to explore new spots.

The Los Angeles Italian Festival

During Italian Heritage Month (October), this fest at Hollywood and Highland brings together food, dance, and a Da Vinci kids' corner.

Lunar New Year

The vibrant Chinese American community in Los Angeles commemorates Lunar New Year, which falls in late January or early February, with gusto. You'll find everything from restaurant specials to the annual Golden Dragon Parade in Chinatown.

Regarding Her Food

Every March, this organization, also known as Re:Her, organizes ten days of special menus and collaborations for female chefs and female-owned restaurants as a celebration of Women's History Month.

Smorgasburg LA

On Sundays, the Row complex in Downtown LA becomes ground zero for more than fifty up-and-coming food vendors at this free-to-enter, rain-or-shine open-air market.

Thai Town Night Market

Head to the 99 Cent Store in Hollywood on Monday and Tuesday nights to taste some of the best Thai street food the city has to offer.

Uncorked LA

Wine lovers should keep an eye out for this massive event at the California Science Center in Exposition Park featuring more than one hundred wineries, food trucks, and more.

THREE ANGELENO-APPROVED OVERNIGHT TRIPS

By Lesley Suter

Some people spend their whole lives dreaming of the day they can come to LA—landing here is often the culmination of a lifelong goal, the reward for years of hard work and dedication. But, once settled, it doesn't take long to realize the allure of getting out of town. Luckily, part of the charm of this place is its proximity to other ones—smaller or beachier or more desert-y locations—to sate whatever a wandering soul might crave, for the price of a tank of gas. Here, three acclaimed Angelenos who understand the power of a quick getaway share their favorite nearby destinations. Make it a day trip, make it a weekend, but whatever you do, make it a great meal.

DAY TRIP 1:
Yucca Valley

by Ellen Bennett

Ellen Bennett is the founder and CEO of Hedley & Bennett. You know those ampersand-labeled aprons every restaurant chef and aspirational home cook has strapped to their torsos? That's her. Born and raised in LA, Bennett moved to Mexico City at eighteen to explore her heritage before returning home to work in some of LA's top kitchens. Now, in addition to being a tycoon in the world of kitchen and work wear, she is also a published author, a mother, and, more recently, a vacation rental owner, having spent much of 2021 fixing up a sweet 750-square-foot home near the high desert community of Yucca Valley, near Joshua Tree, California.

"It's a very different type of desert vibe than Palm Springs," says Bennett of the destination surrounding Joshua Tree National Park, where the landscape is dominated by the namesake towering cactus and endless vistas of alien rock formations. "I love that you can drive two hours away from LA and it's like you're on another planet. I go out there, sit in a hammock, and just read a book and look off into the desert mountains. It's very calm and chill."

Which is not to say there isn't also plenty of activity. Over the past several years, high desert areas like Joshua Tree, Pioneer Town, Yucca Valley, and Twentynine Palms have seen a surge in tourism, and with it, a wave of new food, drink, and recreation options that complement the region's old-timey landmarks and signature rustic, off-the-grid vibe.

Here, check out Bennett's picks for where to eat, drink, and shop in California's high desert.

For stocking up

The Dez Fine Food
61705 29 Palms Highway, Joshua Tree

Grocery options out in this part of the desert are limited, so often what we'll do is stop along the way out from LA at one of the Whole Foods or Trader Joe's along the route for our main staples. Once we're in town, though, there's the Dez, a cute gourmet shop where you can get really nice organic sandwiches and baked goods and coffee, but also Fly by Jing chili crisp and other pantry essentials. It's great for picnic supplies, too—grab a salad or a sandwich to take into the park.

For pastries and breakfast

Luna Bakery
55700 29 Palms Highway, Yucca Valley

Luna is a great organic bakery with breads, pastries, sandwiches, and salads. They have amazing focaccia, but pretty much everything here is wonderful. You can't go wrong.

For the hottest lunch in town

La Copine
848 Old Woman Springs Road, Yucca Valley

La Copine feels like a miracle oasis in the desert, like it shouldn't be here, but somehow it is. Everything they serve is very fresh, very organic, very flavorful—just effortless California cooking, and the whole vibe is very high-low in a way that's very fitting in the desert. You're like, "Wow, I'm having duck-fat potatoes and biodynamic wine. But then I'm also having grits, and everyone is covered in dirt and in hiking clothes." It's a total scene, and nearly impossible to get reservations. You just have to walk in and try your best.

For afternoon tacos and margs

The Red Dog Saloon
53539 Mane Street, Pioneertown

Right on the main strip in old Pioneer Town is the Red Dog Saloon. It's an actual old saloon that was redone and is now a great place to come to eat or grab a drink. Chef Ari Kolender is behind the food, and everything is so friggin' good, but especially the tacos. Everything is so fresh, from the salsa to the guacamole. The whole Old West town feels like a movie set, and there are big outdoor picnic tables and string lights, and it has this wonderful hipster energy. It's a perfect surprise in the middle of the desert.

For pizza

Pie for the People
58960 29 Palms Highway, Yucca Valley

Pie for the People is legit, delicious pizza. They put a little semolina at the bottom for some crunch, and then the top is soft and squishy, almost like mochi. Be sure to order in advance, though, as the wait time can be forty-five minutes to an hour or more.

For cocktails

The Tiny Pony Tavern
57205 29 Palms Highway, Yucca Valley

The Tiny Pony Tavern has modern bar food and truly great drinks—not just beer but proper cocktails, too, like a Pickletini and Frozen Painkiller.

For biker bar vibes and hearty food

Pappy & Harriet's Pioneertown Palace
53688 Pioneertown Road, Pioneertown

Pappy & Harriet's has been around for what seems like forever—it's definitely an institution. You'll pull up and see one hundred Harleys parked outside, but it's more than just a biker bar. You walk inside and it's a mash-up of people: hippies, moms and dads, young hipsters, kids, and actual bikers. They're all just hanging out together eating burgers and drinking beer. It's also a great live music venue; whoever books it has been getting some really interesting acts. It's a great place to go at night and catch a show and have a drink.

For wine and gifts

Wine & Rock Shop
59006 29 Palms Highway, Yucca Valley

There was a store in LA that I loved called Individual Medley, and it had incredible gifts. During COVID, they closed down and moved to Joshua Tree to run the Wine & Rock shop, and now it's where we always stop for good wine on our way into town—and rocks! The quality of stuff they have, you just can't find anywhere else out here, with lots of organic, biodynamic, and natural wines. Then they also have gourmet snacks and fancy dry goods, like Rancho Gordo beans. The rest is just incredibly tasteful, arty gifts.

For the ultimate sunset

Joshua Tree National Park

The park itself is a stunner and honestly the reason we fully fell in love with this area. If you think the landscape driving into Joshua Tree is beautiful, going into the actual park is absolutely baffling. You've got gigantic rocks and cliffs all over the place and these perfect, pristine Joshua trees everywhere. It feels

like Jurassic Park in a way, so foreign and untouched and beautiful. We've done photo shoots there, we've done picnics there, we've gone on a ton of hikes—you can make it a big one or you can make it a short one. I have a little Mini Cooper convertible and I just love driving to the park with the top down, especially toward the end of the day, when the sun is setting. Just blast some delicious music and you're like, "Okay, this is awesome."

DAY TRIP 2: San Diego
by Mario Lopez

Yes, *that* Mario Lopez. Bayside heartthrob A. C. Slater himself—and, more recently, the charming host of everything from *Access Hollywood* to his own iHeart radio show, *On with Mario Lopez*. But before all that, Lopez grew up a first-generation Mexican American in a heavily Latino neighborhood of San Diego—or, as he'll describe it, "America's finest city." "It's the official slogan for a reason," says Lopez, who adores his hometown and gets back as often as he can to go on taco crawls, hang with family,

and border hop to eat spiny lobsters near Tijuana. "All I do is eat when I go down there—it's amazing."

The city's appeal as a destination goes beyond food, though. "San Diego has the most perfect climate ever," says Lopez. "It's always seventy-five. And because of the naval base and its proximity to Mexico, it's just a really diverse culture down there." "Down there" is in reference to San Diego's being a scenic two-hour drive south of LA, a trip thousands of Angelenos make each weekend to hit the beach, stroll the trendy Gaslamp Quarter, and eat their fill of some of the best Mexican food in the country.

Here are Lopez's favorite spots to eat, drink, and play in and around San Diego.

For mariscos
Karina's Seafood
Multiple locations

There's no better place in the US for mariscos, or Mexican-style seafood, than San Diego. In other places, you order a shrimp cocktail, and you get like four shrimp. Here, you'll get an enormous goblet of huge, fresh jumbo shrimp in lime juice with cucumber and chile. It's a whole other experience. Karinas is my favorite place to get mariscos in town. There used to be just one location, but it blew up and now there are several all throughout San Diego. Everything here is just delicious and authentic, and there's also live music and drinks, so it's a really fun atmosphere, too.

For tacos

Tacos El Gordo
511 F Street, San Diego

There are a million places to get tacos in San Diego, but this is my family's favorite. It started off as this little stand, but now it's a restaurant where you can get excellent tacos made with tripe, lengua (tongue), beef cheek—all kinds of tacos, not just chicken. I love to eat it all. It sounds wild, but it's absolutely delicious.

For breakfast

Morning Glory
550 West Date Street, San Diego

I love coming here for breakfast. They have these amazing soufflé pancakes and baked skillet pancakes, and a bunch of crazy omelets and other dishes. Besides the incredible food, it's the most Instagrammable breakfast spot in SD.

For nightlife

Gaslamp Quarter and Little Italy Crawl

The whole Gaslamp Quarter downtown is very clean and nice, with new restaurants and bars

opening all the time. It's a good place to spend a night out just sort of wandering in and out of all the little bars. My buddy opened up this Italian spot down there called **Lavo** that's really great. Little Italy is right downtown, too, which is a cute area to walk around with some really nice restaurants, including steak houses like **Animae** and **Born and Raised**.

For a historic stay

Hotel del Coronado
1500 Orange Avenue, Coronado

I love doing a quick weekend getaway with my wife, and we'll often head down to Coronado. Coronado is this little island that's connected to San Diego via a famous giant bridge that you can see from Downtown, and there's a historic hotel there that's just beautiful. There's a lot of history—Marilyn Monroe used to stay there—and apparently some of the rooms are haunted. Today, the hotel has a great restaurant, and it's right on a gorgeous beach. Even if you don't stay there, it's worth wandering through the building to admire the architecture.

For a worthy side trip
**Puerto Nuevo and
the Valle de Guadalupe**
The border into Mexico is right there, and so I go all the time to eat tacos and mariscos, and then hit Puerto Nuevo for some of the best lobster in the world. It's literally this lobster village, with people who have converted their homes into restaurants. They catch lobsters that day, you point out what you want, and they cook it for you right there. It's incredible.

From there, depending on traffic, the Valle is another hour's drive south from San Diego, and it's this amazing well-kept secret. It's like a little Napa Valley, with incredible wineries, restaurants, and hotels. My sister got married down there, and we had the best time. By far the nicest place to stay in Valle de Guadalupe is **El Cielo**, where they offer these luxurious suites. For very good wine and a great atmosphere, go to **Decantos Vinícola**. They sometimes have live music playing, and it's the perfect place for a daylong outing with family and friends. The food in general is amazing in all of Valle de Guadalupe, but **Fauna** is one of the best. They are not afraid to take risks with a really experimental menu.

DAY TRIP 3:
Los Alamos
by Nyesha Arrington

Chef Nyesha Arrington is about as California as it gets. Born and raised in and around LA to a multicultural family of artists and musicians, she has a demeanor and a cooking style that ooze with sunny, only-in-California ease. And while her formal training leans French, it's how she applies that flair to the acclaimed produce of her home state that's earned her a reputation as one of SoCal's best chefs. But while she's spent her whole life here, she only recently stumbled upon what's become her favorite weekend destination: the rustic, sleepy, wine-fueled town of Los Alamos—part of the greater Santa Ynez Valley wine region.

Crest over the craggy mountains that hug the eastern edge of Santa Barbara, and you dip into another world—this is horse country, farm country, wine country, and, increasingly, food country. "Los Alamos is just really cute in that quintessential, country-esque kind of way," says Arrington. "It's a really slow town, and it's the kind of place where you can go for a day or two and make multiple great stops along the way." A short two-hour drive north of LA, the Santa Ynez region has seen a boom in tourism over the last decade or so, since it featured prominently in the indie hit film *Sideways*. "The first time I visited was for a food event, and friends kept sending me recommendations of places to check out while I was up there," says Arrington. "I was like, 'Wow, this place has so much to offer.'" Since then, she's gone back again and again, racking up her own list of must-hit spots for every type of visitor.

Here, then, are Arrington's picks for where to eat, drink, lounge, and stay in the central-coast wine town of Los Alamos:

For the can't-miss meal
Bell's
406 Bell Street, Los Alamos

I think what really solidified this whole area for me is Bell's. The first time I went was right before the pandemic, so they were fairly new, but I just remember having this impeccable tasting-menu meal out on the patio. The menu is very French—I'm classically French trained, so that always kind of speaks to me—but it's not pretentious at all. It feels very "Franch" vibes, y'know? Welcoming, with zero pretension, and then the food is executed at an extremely high level.

For breakfast
Bob's Well Bread
550 Bell Street, Los Alamos

Generally, where I would love to start every day is at Bob's Well Bread for some coffee and incredible, incredible pastries. The lines can be long in the morning, but it's definitely worth it, and they have a wide variety of options for everyone—not just pastries but full breakfast, too. I love to sit outside in the courtyard area, where they have this really amazing garden, and just enjoy the perfect weather. Bob himself was a former Hollywood executive and recreational baker. He decided to get out of the business and open this shop up here, and now he's living the dream. You can feel it.

To stay
Skyview Los Alamos
9150 US-101, Los Alamos

Not too far from Bob's Well Bread is the Skyview Los Alamos motel—this super-cute, retro motel that's been recently renovated and is now a popular place to stay. I'll spend the night here, then go for a run in the morning and end at Bob's for breakfast. You know how some hotels can feel really structured? This one feels very warm and casual, and it's so scenic—you can see all of Santa Barbara from the pool. I'll sometimes spend half the day hanging out at the hotel, sipping wine, and enjoying the view.

For a hike and a picnic
Los Alamos County Park

In 2018, I began to prioritize fitness a lot more. Before that, it was always about working in kitchens and then eating dinner late and not prioritizing my health—it was stressful. Now I try to think about those things more, so even on vacation I try to get some sort of athleticism every day. Luckily there are so many amazing hiking trails around here. My favorite one starts at Los Alamos County Park, where there are a bunch of great trails for hiking or running, but there are also a lot of tables there if you wanted to have a picnic, too. It's just a really nice setting.

To drink
Rideau Vineyard
1562 Alamo Pintado Road, Solvang

There's a whole Santa Ynez wine trail up here, and you could spend days going from one winery to another. No matter what, though, I feel like at least one middle-of-the-day wine tasting is required. I always make sure I visit a vineyard called Rideau—they make really excellent wines, and it's Black-owned, which is important to me. I always buy a few bottles to take home.

For chasing windmills
Solvang

Los Alamos is part of this whole area with a few little towns close by, including Los Olivos and Solvang. Solvang looks like an adorable old German town, with several windmills and Tudor-style buildings. There are a bunch of traditional German-style bakeries here, which are great. And because I'm such a clog person in the kitchen, the last time I was there I stopped into a clog store and bought some real wood ones. I still wear them!

For lunch or dinner
Bar Le Côte
2375 Alamo Pintado Avenue, Los Olivos

Bar Le Côte is the place to come if you love seafood. My buddy Brad Mathews is the chef and co-owner there, and I've always really enjoyed his food and just how he operates the restaurants. You're really close to Santa Barbara, too, where most of California's best fish comes from, so the quality is just pristine. You aren't ever going to go wrong if you're eating seafood or drinking wine around here, but especially at Bar Le Côte.

HOW TO GET A SEAT AT THE TABLE:

From reservations to walk-ins

By Emma Orlow and Lesley Suter

It wasn't always this way, but lately, getting a reservation in Los Angeles—especially during peak times—can be difficult, verging on impossible. Thankfully, over the years covering LA's dining scene, we've gathered some tips for how to make the most of your time dining out.

Plan ahead

Resy is generally the most-used booking platform for hot new restaurants in LA. Ideally, start making your dining wish list more than one month in advance, as many places allow you to make reservations four weeks out, although this varies considerably. If the restaurant or bar doesn't list what time its books open, call and ask in advance. Then mark your calendar and be sure to set a reminder. If the reservation window opens at ten A.M. or even midnight, log in exactly at that time to try to avoid being disappointed. However, if your ideal spot is already booked, there are a few things you can still do . . .

Get on the wait list

Add yourself to the wait list in OpenTable, Resy, or Tock, if available, and turn on your notifications so you are the first to see when a table opens up that fits your parameters. Angelenos are flaky by reputation, and that's not altogether wrong. Sometimes a restaurant has more reservations available than what's put into the apps. It's worth emailing or calling the restaurant directly to see if they can squeeze you in.

Walk in

Likewise, plenty of restaurants leave space for walk-ins (you can even ask them what percentage of the restaurant they leave for walk-ins to better gauge your chances). If you don't have a reservation, you'll have the most luck as a walk-in going alone—a seat at the bar is the easiest spot in a restaurant to get. If you want to stop by with a group, make sure you're

picking a restaurant that didn't just open, and therefore isn't going to have the hype machine drumming up crowds. But generally, the best time to hit a restaurant without a reservation is when the spot first opens, either eating with the early birds or putting your name down for later and getting a drink to fill up the hours-long wait. Or try later in the evening, past the prime-time rush.

Try no-reservation spots

A handful of restaurants in LA don't take reservations—Jitlada in East Hollywood, Capri Club in Eagle Rock, and Sushi Gen in Little Tokyo are a few of them.

Mostly, just be flexible and have an open mind. Try a place that was buzzy two years ago instead of right this moment. And if you don't get into your hit-list place, there are thousands of other wonderful and surprising places you can try.

WHERE TO EAT NEAR MAJOR TOURIST ATTRACTIONS

Chances are you're not only coming to LA to eat: We've got fantastic museums, world-class concert venues, and some of the best museums in the country here, too. Still, doing a tourist activity doesn't need to mean eating like a tourist when you're in LA. Here's where to eat near major tourist destinations.

Dodger Stadium

Yes, outside food is permitted; check out the Dodgers' website for the full details and rules.

▶ El Ruso (page 136)

▶ Quarter Sheets Pizzeria (page 38)

Hollywood Bowl

▶ Clark Street Diner (page 89)

▶ Hui Tou Xiang
1643 North Cahuenga Boulevard, Hollywood
Head to this outpost of an SGV legend for a quick bite before a show. The gigantic hui tou dumplings are a must as are the pork leek pancakes.

Hollywood Walk of Fame

▶ Luv2eat Thai Bistro (page 90)

▶ The Musso & Frank Grill (page 91)

Hollywood Forever Cemetery

▶ Mush Bakery
5224 Sunset Boulevard, Hollywood
Head to this walk-up bakery for traditional Armenian pastries like borek and meaty lahmnajune, flatbreads topped with spiced beef.

▶ Providence (page 92)

The Huntington Library

▶ Golden Deli (page 12)

▶ Pie 'n Burger (page 14)

Getty Center

▶ Anzu
11270 La Grange Avenue, Sawtelle
Sawtelle isn't far from the scenic Getty Center; there are tons of options there, but for quick and casual, an order of Anzu's chicken karaage hits the spot.

▶ Pizzana (page 92)

Griffith Observatory

▶ Kismet (page 36)

▶ Little Dom's
2128 Hillhurst Avenue, Los Feliz
A Los Feliz favorite among locals and celebs, this chic Italian spot offers sandwiches during the day and pricey (but always filling) red-sauce entrees at night.

▶ Northern Thai Food Club
5301 Sunset Boulevard, East Hollywood
It's a nearly straight shot from Thai Town up to the observatory, making this all-day buffet the perfect starting place. Don't skip the kao soi or the sai oua sausage.

LACMA / La Brea Tar Pits / Academy Museum

▶ Meals by Genet
1053 South Fairfax Avenue, Little Ethiopia
One of the standouts in Little Ethiopia, Meals by Genet boasts beautiful injera and must-try doro wot, a chicken stew that takes chef Genet Agonafer three days to make.

▶ République (page 92)

MOCA / The Broad Museum / Walt Disney Concert Hall

▶ Grand Central Market (page 67)

▶ Otium (page 69)

The Rose Bowl

▶ Ramen Tatsynoya
16 North Fair Oaks Avenue, Pasadena
An import from Fukuoka, Japan, this ramen shop focuses on tonkotsu (pork broth) and proprietary noodles.

▶ Roma Market (page 14)

Santa Monica Pier

▶ Blue Plate Oysterette
1355 Ocean Avenue, Santa Monica
Lobster rolls, prawn cocktails, and oysters on the half shell just a stroll from the pier? What could be better?

▶ Crudo e Nudo (page 146)

▶ Hot Dog on a Stick
1633 Ocean Front Walk, Santa Monica
A pier mainstay for more than 75 years, this aptly named institution serves tourists their choice of turkey, vegetarian, or beef wieners with tall paper cups of lemonade.

Venice Beach

▶ Felix (page 147)

▶ Hinano Cafe (page 148)

Watts Towers Art Center

▶ Hawkins House of Burgers (page 128)

▶ Jim Dandy Fried Chicken
11328 Vermont Avenue, South LA
This South LA icon is the standard bearer for fried chicken in town. Round out your meal with the corn fritters, which come dusted with powdered sugar.

ACKNOWLEDGMENTS

Thank you to the Eater team behind this book, who took their love of the Los Angeles food scene and turned it into an insightful, exciting guide to the city—particularly Cathy Chaplin and Karen Palmer, who wrote the listings. Thank you to Britt Aboutaleb and Amanda Kludt for bringing this idea to life, to Ellie Krupnick for keeping us all on track, to Nat Belkov for the design collaboration, to Erin Russell for fact-checking, and to Lesley Suter and Stephanie Wu for being the guiding forces. Thank you to Vox Media's Eric Karp and Hilary Sharp for literally making the deal happen, and to Aude White and Dane McMillan for making sure people know about it.

Thank you to Laura Dozier and Diane Shaw at Abrams for teaching all of us how to make a guidebook! And for their patience on a project with so many cooks. Thank you to Natasha Martin, Mamie Sanders, and Danielle Kolodkin at Abrams for their enthusiastic publicity and marketing efforts.

And most importantly, thank you to the sensational writers, editors, reporters, illustrators, and designers who have contributed to Eater LA over the past several years; this book would not have been possible without your passion and your enduring work.

CONTRIBUTORS

Hillary Dixler Canavan is Eater's restaurant editor and the author of the publication's debut book, *Eater: 100 Essential Restaurant Recipes from the Authority on Where to Eat and Why It Matters* (Abrams). She lives in Los Angeles with her husband and daughter.

Cathy Chaplin, a James Beard Award–nominated journalist, is a senior editor at Eater LA and the author of *Food Lovers' Guide to Los Angeles*. She lives in Altadena.

Martha Cheng is the food editor at *Honolulu Magazine*, the author of *The Poke Cookbook*, and a writer for national publications.

For more than eight years, **Farley Elliott** was the senior editor for Eater LA, with a focus on breaking news, big features, and LA's sprawling underground dining scene. He won some awards and even wrote a book on the history of Los Angeles street food, which you should read.

Matthew Kang is the lead editor of Eater LA and has covered dining, restaurants, food culture, and nightlife in Los Angeles for more than fourteen years. His work has been featured in *Angeleno* magazine and on Taste. Matthew hosted a YouTube show called K-Town covering Korean food in America for Eater and has been featured on Netflix's *Street Food*, Hulu's *Searching for Soul Food*, and Cooking Channel's *Food: Fact or Fiction*.

Emma Orlow is a reporter for Eater NY covering restaurants, bars, pop-ups, and the people powering them. She was born and raised in New York City and has freelanced for the *New York Times, GrubStreet, Bon Appétit*, the *Los Angeles Times*, and more. She loves vintage 1970s cookbooks, Jell-O, and good ol' fashioned tuna melts.

Karen Palmer is a Los Angeles–based food writer and editor with twenty-plus years of experience. In addition to working closely with the Eater LA team, her work has been featured in *Travel + Leisure, Food & Wine, Los Angeles Magazine*, and many others. A New Jersey native and pizza obsessive, Karen is the founder of a French-bread pizza pop-up called Pain Pizza.

Lesley Suter has been an editor on the national team of Eater since 2018, starting as the travel editor and moving up to special-projects editor in 2021. Before that, she served as the food editor at *Los Angeles Magazine* for nine years and cowrote two cookbooks with the chefs behind Bestia and Bavel, and she has been a proud Angeleno for more than two decades.

INDEX

Page references in *italics* refer to illustrations.

Editor: Laura Dozier
Designer: Jenice Kim
Managing Editor: Lisa Silverman
Production Manager: Larry Pekarek

Library of Congress Control Number: 2023945801

ISBN: 978-1-4197-6582-7
eISBN: 978-1-64700-890-1

ABRAMS The Art of Books
195 Broadway, New York, NY 10007
abramsbooks.com